T0209416

CROSS OVER TO THE CROSS

Bringing the Hope of the Cross
to Shia Muslims in Your Community

REV. DR. ELIE HASBANI

WESTBOW
PRESS®
A DIVISION OF THOMAS NELSON
& ZONDERVAN

WestBow Press books may be ordered through booksellers or by contacting:

WestBow Press
A Division of Thomas Nelson & Zondervan
1663 Liberty Drive
Bloomington, IN 47403
www.westbowpress.com
1 (866) 928-1240

ISBN: 978-1-9736-8549-4 (sc)
ISBN: 978-1-9736-8550-0 (e)

Library of Congress Control Number: 2020902863

Print information available on the last page.

WestBow Press rev. date: 03/04/2020

I dedicate this book to the churches committed to the
Gospel engaged in God's mission in the Muslim World
and persecuted people, especially Shi'a Muslims.

CONTENTS

First and foremost, I'd like to thank my beautiful wife, Luna. She not only supported and encouraged me throughout the process of completing this book, but she did so with love and patience. I love her more than I could ever express in words.

Thank you Gina Huff, Gina Kelley, and Pam Weiss, who put effort and time in helping me edit this book.

Lastly, a special thanks to my dear friend and brother in Christ, Jim Borris, for his financial support. He not only believed in my mission but encouraged me to share this book with you.

PREFACE

God loves all of humanity, and that includes Muslims. He has blessed me with a special heart to see Shi'a Muslims receive the atoning work of God through Jesus Christ. Once my closest friends in my native Lebanon, I had opportunities all around me to share the gospel with them and witnessed many come to Christ.

When I moved to the US, I saw that thousands and thousands of Muslims had also emigrated from the Middle East. Muslims, including many Shi'a, were my neighbors once again. God showed me that I didn't need to cross an ocean to reach Muslims; there was an active mission field right here, in my own backyard. It is a mission field free from many of the restrictions and the persecutions that came with openly evangelizing in Muslim countries.

My heart's desire is to share this revelation with the western church that has a preconception that, in order to "do missions," one must raise funds and board an airplane with a passport in hand. The reality is that, as Christians, our mission field is where our feet are at any given moment, and that there are even more opportunities to share the gospel with those around us than there are overseas. But sadly, even some of those who grasp this are not motivated to go. The harvest is plenty, but the workers are few. Some Christians are too busy. Some feel they aren't "ready." Others have prejudices against Muslims, especially these days, when one can't turn on the news without hearing about atrocities taking place in the Middle East or attacks on innocent people in the name of Islam. This has created fear in many hearts that the enemy has used to sideline us and created distance between Christians and their Muslim neighbors and coworkers.

That said, there are a growing number of believers who have a desire to share their faith with the growing number of Muslims around them, but their efforts are hindered by their lack of knowledge of culture and beliefs. Although Muslims in the US are generally far more open than they would have been in their own countries to learn about Christianity, many in the Church aren't even sure where to begin. I am also seeing more and more believers genuinely seeking to learn more about Muslims with the rise of radical political beliefs.

This book is comprised of a collection of four parts, each covering unique, but related content and together, creating a practical tool for Christians to reach and disciple Shi'a Muslims for Christ. Each chapter is followed by group discussion questions to provoke thought and action. The content can be easily modified for reaching all Muslims and with general evangelism.

This series of four parts, Cross Over to the Cross, was designed to address this very need and to overcome the personal, spiritual, political, and cultural obstacles that are preventing the western church from effectively evangelizing to Muslims, with a special emphasis on the Shi'a people.

My goal is to:

- Help Christians recognize God's heart for Muslims.
- Provide a tool to put in the hands of Christians mobilizes and equips them to reach Shi'a Muslims.
- Encourage believers and help them understand that it's easy and that they can do it!
- Highlight the incredible opportunity that exists here in the US to evangelize to Shi'a Muslims with our freedom of speech and the ability to share without persecution often seen in other parts of the world.
- See churches build trust and move to love, integrate, and disciple new Shi'a Muslim coverts to Christ, lifting them up onto their level.
- Break down walls by sharing the history of the Shi'a, culture, and tenets of Shi'a Islam.
- And, most importantly, to share specific methods for effective evangelizing and discipling.

God will use individuals, ministries, and churches to forward the Great Commission. God is not limited in how he will accomplish this. There is no formula, but it is my hope that these serve as inspiration and a starting point to reach the Shi'a Muslims living and working among us in the US.

I pray that a bright light would shine on the wonderful truth of the cross and that the church would rise as Christ's ambassadors, as though God were making his appeal through us (2 Corinthians 5:20), for if Shi'a Muslims understand the core of the faith and understand redemption, they will come to faith in large numbers. It is these Shi'a who will, in turn, share with others in both the US and in their home countries, and through this, can ultimately change the world!

INTRODUCTION

With all the unsaved people in the world, some may ask why I am focusing on Shi'a Muslims. First, understand that first and foremost, my prayer is that these books will help Christian believers understand that their mission field can be right where they stand and that the opportunities are plentiful. I encourage each of you to stop and pray for the person in front of you as the Holy Spirit leads, regardless of nationality or background. And second, although these books are focused on the background and strategy to lead Muslim Shi'a to the cross and share Christ's redemption, the approach can easily be modified for reaching Muslims and with evangelism in general.

That said, growing up in Beirut, Lebanon, and in the south of Lebanon among the Shi'a communities, has given me deep insight into their unique culture and beliefs as well as a heart to see them come to salvation. I have come to find that Christians have much in common with the Shi'a. In fact, there are many more things that unite us than that separate us. The Shi'a identity, culture, society, traditions, and even some of their beliefs are more similar to Christianity than their Sunni cousins.

Islam is comprised of two primary sects: Sunni and Shi'a, with the minority being the Shi'a, representing only 15–20 percent of all Muslims, or approximately 300 million worldwide. Although their numbers are small in the US today, there is a growing population of Shi'a Muslims—some statistics showing close to one million—with larger concentrations in and around Dearborn, Los Angeles, Boston, New York, Dallas, Nashville, Chicago and Milwaukee. There is ample opportunity to reach the Shi'a in our own backyards. Although more and more Shi'a Muslims are coming to Christ each day through dreams and visions, I believe that Christians are the real instrument God is going to use to win the lost, help them to grow, protect them, bring light into their darkness, and destroy the evil around them.

The information presented in the book was developed not only through extensive research in conjunction with my personal experiences, but also through conversations and interviews with countless churches, ministries, pastors, and Shi'a Muslims. Within these volumes, we will cover the history of Islam including the Sunni/Shi'a split, culture, and tradition, and effective evangelism, as well as tackling such topics and questions as:

- Is Jesus the real imam who redeemed the Shi'a?
- Difficulty many Christians have with sharing the core of the gospel and how to effectively share the truth of the cross with Shi'a.
- Helping Christians who are struggling with evangelism.
- Building effective approaches to reaching Shi'a Muslims one-on-one and in church settings.
- Disunity between churches, ministries, and pastors, and the importance of gaining input and learning from Christian workers.
- Addressing the debate as to whether we should bring Muslims to church.

I encourage you to use these four parts as study guides in small groups. I have included discussion questions within each chapter to prompt discussion, prayer, and action.

My prayer for readers: I will continually ask our Father in heaven to fill you with knowledge of his will through the wisdom and understanding that the Holy Spirit gives you, peace and love to live a life worthy for Christ Jesus, and to empower you to testify about his redemption among Muslims.

PART ONE

This first chapter reminds the reader, presumably a Christian believer, of our collective call to help fulfill the Great Commission. I seek to address the question of what it takes to effectively equip Christians for mission and evangelism with a specific focus on reaching Muslims. A compelling personal testimony is included in this chapter with the intention of connecting with the reader (in that I once was fearful and hesitant to share Christ with others), but also to illustrate that there is good fruit that comes from taking bold steps in faith.

This chapter also overviews reasons for evangelizing to Muslim. It seeks to remind the reader of God's love for ALL people, including Muslims. In a time when stories about radical Islam and terror attacks can be seen regularly in the media with fear and misconceptions running rampant, my desire it to bring things back to a human level. Islam is an ideology, whereas Muslims are people; people who like us, are in need of a savior. They are no more or less deserving to hear and accept the Good News as we were prior to our salvation. Additionally, this chapter begins to touch on the roots of the Islamic faith so that the reader has some understanding of the origins of the faith in the context of the Muslim predisposition.

Finally, this chapter overviews the responsibility of the believer in effective evangelism in the form of a set of principles that create a solid foundation in which to move forward in reaching Muslims for Christ. Principles include; knowing who God is, knowing your identify in Him, incarnational living, a shift away from the "I" mentality that is so prevalent today, building relational bridges, understanding how God uses the body of Christ to fulfill the Great Commission, and the power of prayer.

Chapter two helps the reader understand reasons why they may find it difficult to evangelize to Muslims, or, why they might feel fear. I tackle common misconceptions as well as valid obstacles that may hinder, but certainly should not prevent us from, effective evangelism. This includes spiritual, cultural, historical, psychological, political and personal reasons as well as ways to overcome and mobilize.

This chapter brings us into a deeper understanding of the Islamic faith, the Shia/Sunni split, Islamic movements and ideologies, the Muslim understanding of salvation, Jesus and Islam, Muslim culture, faith struggles and questions Muslims (particularly those who have emigrated outside of their communities) have, Muslim views on women and much more. This is done not to create barriers but instead to create an understanding and see commonalities in which to build bridges upon.

CHAPTER 1
THE GREAT COMMISSION

All Christians should be equipped to further the work of Christ, and I believe they should be motivated by love to share their faith with Muslims. In this chapter, I am answering one question: how do we equip Christians for mission and evangelism to Muslims? I hope that in sharing my personal experiences and observations, this book will motivate you, the reader, to be a brave part of God's mission to bring others, including Shia Muslims, to Christ.

To be effective, we must often first have work done in our own hearts and minds for God to utilize us for his purposes. The following story helps to illustrate my passion for sharing the message of Jesus to Muslims and describes the work God needed to do in my heart for me to begin. This experience was a stepping-stone for my life's efforts to bring others to Jesus.

During my time at discipleship training school in Limassol, Cyprus, from 1987 to 1989, I joined a team established for street evangelism. Every day, we went out into the streets to meet with people and tell them about Jesus Christ. On Fridays, we would pray the whole day and then, late in the afternoon, go out and do a street event. We would start by worshipping through music and, as people gathered around us, some of the team members would perform a short play about sin and its terrible consequences; the rest of the team would pray for the people, asking God to open their hearts to accept his word.

One day during the play, I asked God to lead me to someone to talk to about the salvation Jesus offers. I was drawn to a man who looked like an Arab. As I began to walk toward him, I became quite nervous. Shaking inside, I prayed for direction on what to do. These words came to my mind: "Do not be afraid; have courage, for I am with you" and "Open your mouth and I will fill it with words." I moved forward, stood by the man, and said simply, "Good play, isn't it?"

"Yes," he said, "but I didn't understand anything. They are talking about Christ, aren't they? They are trying to fool all these people."

I wanted to disagree, to shout *No, we are telling the truth*, but instead, I said, "No. Where are you from?" even though I already knew from his accent that he was from Lebanon.

"I'm from Lebanon," he answered.

"Where in Lebanon?"

"From the south of Lebanon. From Tyre," he answered.

"I am from the south too. What is your name?"

"Mohammed," he replied.

Suddenly, my tongue got tangled in my mouth and I couldn't speak. This man was a Muslim. Millions of thoughts ran through my mind before I was able to speak again. You see, I had much bitterness in my heart toward Muslims! Many are my enemies from wartime. Is salvation for them as well? I was not ready to give him the message of peace and tell him about the cross of Jesus Christ. I forgot I was standing before someone who had the same need for salvation as I once had. The only thing I could think about was my hatred for him. I did not care if he was saved or not!

Mohammed broke my train of thought when he asked, "What part of the south are you from?"

"Deir Mimas," I replied. And from that, he knew I was a Christian. He asked me if I was with this group, and I answered that I was. He continued to press me on why we were doing this. Why were we evangelizing on the street? What did we want to tell these people?

I felt attacked and was speechless, but then I realized he was coming right out and asking me to tell him about the good news in Jesus Christ! But I was not ready to tell him anything, so I decided to move away. "Thank you, Mohammed. Nice meeting you," I said and turned my back.

Then the Holy Spirit began to talk to me. *You promised me that you would share your story of how I saved you. This was your opportunity, but you didn't use it.* At that moment, I decided to go back and share my story with

Mohammad. I approached him, but fear and hatred again overpowered me. I didn't even want to look at his face. I pressed on, despite these strong feelings.

I simply asked him if I could share with him how the Lord saved and changed me. I did not want to get into a controversial theological discussion about doctrine—I just wanted him to hear my story. He was fully attentive and interested. I did not know what was going on inside of him until I noticed that he was crying. Then he said to me, "I need this Christ you are talking about." I told him he could ask Jesus to come into his life right then, right there. I explained that Jesus was there with us and was willing to save him from his sins, just as he had done for me. I heard Mohammed say, "Jesus, I believe in you as the Son of God. You died on the cross to save me. Please forgive my sins and come into my life and free me!"

I could not believe what was happening. This was the first person I was brave enough to share my story with. The first one to give his life to Christ was an enemy of mine. God opened my eyes to see that there was a big difference between Islam and Muslims. Muslims, just like me, need God's love and redemption from their sins and needed salvation. Islam is an ideology, teaching against the cross and the Son of God, Jesus Christ. Islam shouldn't be confused with Muslims.

From that moment on, Mohammed and I shared the same goal, the same future, and the same salvation. His conversion was a turning point in my life regarding my relationship with Muslims. God was showing me his great love for all humanity and how I could love them too. My heart was changing. God had answered my prayers; I had a new inner strength to forgive.

After this, Mohammed and I developed a friendship. We met regularly, prayed together, read the Bible, and even worshipped together. The walls I had built between my enemies and me had been broken down. I was given the chance to confess to him my hatred and that I was wrong. I asked him to forgive me for all the hatred and bitterness I harbored. My hatred was replaced with God's love. This was not an easy step. It takes a work of grace and the power of the Holy Spirit in one's life to heal the wounds of the past and turn from hatred to forgiveness and loving your enemies. Jesus had given me a powerful experience so I could understand what he meant when he said, "You have heard that it was said: Love your neighbor and hate your enemy. But I tell you, love your enemies and pray for those who persecute you, that you may be children of your Father in heaven" (Matthew 5:43–45a, NIV).

So much of my youth, all my experiences in civil war, the daily reality of walking with only one real leg—these all told me that I should hate Muslims. Now I was being taught by God that, although Islam may be a false religion that can lead to so much error and violence, Muslims are people he loves and longs to save just as he had done for me. I understood that God wanted me to have compassion for people whether they were Muslims or Buddhists or Jews. I began to understand the impact evil had to imprison the lives and hearts of people of all backgrounds and religions. I came to understand the biblical teaching that the battle is not against flesh and blood but against spiritual wickedness. He wanted me to see clearly and to understand the great commission and power of the gospel, through the Holy Spirit, to save. "Then Jesus came to them and said, 'All authority in heaven and on earth has been given to me. Therefore go and make disciples of all nations, baptizing them in the name of the Father and of the Son and of the Holy Spirit, and teaching them to obey everything I have commanded you. And surely I am with you always, to the very end of the age'" (Matthew 28:18–20, NIV).

Reasons for Evangelizing Muslims

There are many reasons that could be given for Christians to reach out to Muslims, but surely the following biblical declarations are enough for us to move forward and share the gospel of Jesus Christ with them.

A wonderful reason God loves Muslims is because, like all humans, they are created in the image of God (Genesis 1:26–27, NIV). Muslims are people like us, created in God's image. We must base our ministries to Muslims upon God's perspective and the value he places on humanity. Most Muslims are concerned about the same things you and I are. They are concerned about their lives here and after. They are worried for their destinies and futures. They want to raise their children well; they are concerned about rising crime and pornography; and they work hard to pay their bills and to survive. Today, Muslims are the white field and plentiful harvest that Jesus talks about in Luke 4:35–38.

At the risk of oversimplification, I provide this recap of a key difference between Christianity and Islam. Muslims look to Abraham as their forefather (Romans 4:11), and this gives them a historical relationship to Christians. Muslims believe that they are spiritually related to Christians and Jews as descendants of Abraham and Ishmael (Genesis 17:20). God chose Abraham (Isaiah 51:2) and made a covenant with him for the benefit of the nations. Through Abraham, God revealed himself as the Lord, the almighty, and the provider who wants to bless all people, including Muslims, through the faith of Abraham. The Bible speaks specifically about what this line is. In Genesis 12:1–3, we see that this refers to the family of Abraham. As we continue on in Genesis 25:23–33 and 26:1–2, we find that God works on earth through the line of Isaac, and Jacob's name subsequently changes to Israel (Genesis 28:13–15) and passes on to Judah. Later, in Deuteronomy 18: 15, where promises, the Lord your God will raise up for you a prophet like me from among you, from your fellow Israelites. You must listen to him, it says specifically that the prophet would come "from among your own brother" to continue this line to David (2 Samuel 7:4–16; Psalm 89:35–38) and finally be fulfilled in Jesus (Matthew 22:42).

In the Bible, Paul warns us about excessive arguments over genealogies (Titus 3:9). At the same time, it is apparent that Muslims pay close attention to genealogies, particularly that of Muhammad. Muhammad established Islam in Arabia. You can find genealogy information on the internet that shows the physical descendants of Ishmael to Muhammad, via Ishmael's second son, Kedar. Muslims are convinced about this for the purpose of putting Muhammad in the Abrahamic line—Abraham, to Ishmael, to Kedar, and all the way to Muhammad. They all lived in Arabia and rebuilt the black cube "Ka'ba, الكعبة" that the prophet Adam already built. It is recorded in Genesis 21:17, that God heard Ishmael crying in the desert and, speaking of Ishmael, God instructed Hagar, "Arise, lift up the lad, and hold him by the hand; for I will make a great nation of him." Further, verse 20 declares that God was with the lad. The truth is, God still longs to be with the descendants of Ishmael. There are over 1.5 billion Muslims in the world who claim Muhammad's teachings. The issue here is not an accuracy of the physical bloodline, but rather of the spiritual association with Ishmael. The promise to Ishmael is limited to his physical line—that it will be large, but also that it includes a promise that it will be eternal.

This is the point: Isaac is the father of a spiritual nation according to the promise in Galatians 3, and Jesus came through this line. Ishmael, who followed his own evil desires, is the father of a physical nation from Hagar, and Muhammad came through this line. Both Isaac and Ishmael are Abraham's sons. Their father loved them both. Both men buried Abraham after his death (Genesis 25:8). The two equally claim the area of Palestine and Israel. Descendants of both claims to be God's true people and follow a monotheistic faith. And both need God's salvation through Abraham's seed, Jesus Christ.

It is God's desire that Christians intentionally pursue Muslims to share the cross of Jesus, Christ's redemption, and to preach Christ as the Messiah and promised one. "There is neither Jew nor Gentile, neither slave nor free, nor is there male and female, for you are all one in Christ Jesus. If you belong to Christ, then you are Abraham's seed, and heirs according to the promise" (Galatians 3:28–29, NIV). Among us, you are all equal. That is, we are all in a common relationship with Jesus Christ. Pure and simple, all belong to Christ. A division, no matter where it has occurred, is a mistake. Wouldn't you want to know that a mistake has been made?

Another compelling reason to share Christ's message is that Muslims are weary of the dogma of their religion and of how Islam doesn't offer peace and hope for its followers. Many Muslims show a steady rise in spiritual interest in Christ and not Christianity, although that interest is quite undefined. They believe there is a daily, growing desire to know Christ's crucifixion. There is an increase in the number of Muslims who are hungry to know about God's redemption and freedom to work through Jesus (John 8: 30–36). Jesus said, "come to me, all you who are weary and burdened, and I will give you rest ..." (Matthew 11:28, NIV). We are hearing everyday testimonies from Muslims who accepted Christ as their savior and Lord, telling us how hungry they were for the truth and freedom. Muslims are looking for inner peace and for spiritual experiences of all kinds (John 16:27). Muslims are sensitive to God and to spiritual matters. They often speak of how God appears to them through dreams and visions, just like he did to Hagar and Ishmael (Genesis 16:7–10, 21:15–20) and the God-fearer, Cornelius (Acts 10:1–8). Unfortunately, Muslims are lost without the one true God! Another general reason is simply that Christians need to wake up and not lose heart (2 Corinthians

4:1–6). I believe equipping Christians is a part of God's plan and desire to reach out to Muslims. God calls us to leave the ninety-nine righteous sheep and seek the one lost sheep until we find it (Luke 15:4–7).

As Christians living in North America, we can fully exercise our rights and freedoms. Most Muslims have never had a chance to hear about Jesus Christ's redemption on the cross in their own countries. They have been deceived by Islam's teaching. I heard a preacher who works with Muslims say, "Islam is like a cancer; if you don't defeat it, it will defeat you and your society." The battleground has entered the Christian field. The real war is not a war against Muslims; it is a war about truth, value, and freedom. It is a war against the ideologies of Islam, violence, and darkness (Ephesians 6:12).

There is a big difference between the Islamic religion and its people. Islam is a set of doctrines and ideologies, but Muslims are humans in need of God's love. It is Christians' responsibility to share the love of God that was demonstrated on the cross by Christ (Romans 5:8) with those Muslims around us and in our neighborhoods.

The most exiting reason: Jesus is coming soon to rapture his bride, the church. There is no time like the present. If Christians want Jesus to return quickly, then they should be preaching the gospel to the Shi'a. Jesus promised us that this gospel of the kingdom will be preached in the whole world as a testimony to all nations, and then the end will come (Matthew 24:14). Revelation, the last book of the Bible, foretells the end time in which a great multitude from every nation and all tribes and peoples and tongues will stand before the throne of God (Revelation 7:9), purchased by the blood of the Lamb (Revelation 5:9). Muslims who accept Christ need to be among the multitudes standing and gathering around the throne of God. God has chosen to reveal himself, his purpose, and his ways to everyone, and he desires all people to know of Christ's crucifixion and resurrection and to worship him.

Biblical Principles for Reaching Out to Muslims

We are called to share the love of Jesus Christ with Muslims. Christians need to follow eight biblical principles in order to effectively communicate the gospel with Muslims.

The first principle is to know who your God is. Get into an intimate relationship with the Triune God. God revealed Himself through His word. There are numerous passages that teach that God the Father, God the Son, and God the Holy Spirit are One God, but distinct persons and yet each hold the attributes of deity. Biblically, no one knows God without general and specific revelations, and no one can know Jesus as the son of the living God without the father's revelation (Matthew 16: 16–17). No one can say, "Jesus is Lord," except by the Holy Spirit (1 Corinthians 12:3).

Jesus teaches, "If you know me, you know the Father because I am from him and he sent me" (John 7:28–29, NIV). Jesus told Philip that they had seen the father because they had seen him (John 14:9–10). Our mission is to reveal God in Christ and not ourselves and our own methods. Muslims cannot change unless they hear the gospel (Romans 10:14–17) and meet Jesus face to face.

The second principle is to know your identity in Christ. When you understand who you are in Christ, you become more secure and comfortable. The Bible teaches Christians about their true identities. We are empowered by God to be like Christ and therefore to show Christ to the world (Acts 1:8). Christ is a humble servant who loves others in the face of persecution. Your identity in Christ should give you confidence to share that Christ was crucified. You stand on a solid foundation (1 Peter 2: 1–10, NIV). Knowing ourselves in Christ protects us from the sin and all the confusion that comes from Islam. Muslims view Christians as crusaders, pagans (*Mushrekeen*- مشركين) and polytheists. We are consistently reminded in the Bible that we are God's children and are working to share his message of love. One of the richest passages about identity in the Bible is found in Ephesians 1:3-14. According to Ephesians 1, we have been blessed with every spiritual blessing; we have been chosen, adopted, redeemed, forgiven, grace-lavished, and unconditionally loved and accepted. We are pure, blameless and forgiven. We have received the hope of spending eternity with God. When we are in Christ, these aspects of our identity can never be changed by what we do. The verses below are all taken from the NIV version:

- I am a new creation in Christ: the old things are passed away, behold all things are become new (2 Corinthians 5:17).
- I am a family member … a child of the most-high God (1 John 3:1).
- I am a member of God's royal priesthood, a holy and one of his own (1 Peter 2:9).
- I am the temple of the Holy Spirit. (1 Corinthians 6:19).
- I am a joint heir with Christ (Romans 8:17).
- I am protected by God (Psalm 91:23).
- I am in Christ and free from condemnation (Romans 8:1).
- I am secure in Christ and cannot be separated from God (Romans 8:28–29).
- I am established, anointed, and sealed by God (2 Corinthians 1:21–22).
- I have been given power, love, a sound mind, and freedom from fear (2 Timothy 1:7).
- I am being perfected by God (Philippians 1:6).
- I am the salt and light of the world (Matthew 5:13–16).
- I have been chosen and appointed to bear fruit (John 15:16).
- I can do all things through Christ who strengthens me (Philippians 4:13)
- I have everything in Christ, all the blessings (Colossians 1; Ephesians 1:3–14).

The third principle involves incarnational living. The word *incarnation* is used to express the idea of Jesus Christ coming to earth in human form. Theologically, the humanity of Jesus is an important aspect of his earthly life. Jesus is divine (John 1:1; Colossians 1:16), yet he also took on a human body to identify with humanity. He was born of a woman (Matthew 1; Luke 2), ate food, slept, and experienced temptation (Matthew 4:1–11). Like other humans, he displayed human emotions, including anger (Mark 3:5), joy (John 15:11), pain, and sorrow (Matthew 26:37). Jesus also became human as part of his divine plan to die on the cross in our place as a sacrifice (Philippians 2:6–11; Hebrews 9:22). Further, in order to be resurrected, he first had to physically die, which required taking on a physical body. Our salvation completely depends upon Jesus's incarnation to this world in human form. The incarnation of Jesus determines, tells, and delivers the basis for Christian mission. The incarnation of Christ helps us to share the unique message of Jesus Christ with Muslims in ways that are appropriate for their cultural background and lifestyles. Just as Jesus was sent out on mission by the Father, he sends us to preach the gospel to Muslims. It means making daily sacrifices to serve others the way Christ served us. Our mission is God's mission: we are ambassadors of Christ, and we are instruments of God's work. We are priests and trust in the work of the Holy Spirit in the lives of Muslims. We must be incarnate among Muslims because God himself is already incarnate among people before we arrive, preparing their hearts to hear his word and revealing that word to them by the work of the Holy Spirit, and transforming them through the power of the cross.

A fourth guiding principle is that God wants to free Christians from the great "I" and direct them toward others. "Jesus said to his disciples, 'Whoever wants to be my disciple must deny themselves and take up their cross and follow me'" (Matthew 16:24, NIV). He must be God-centered instead of self-centered. Christians must be willing to give up their Christian traditions of pride, prejudice, and lifestyle, and begin to serve by bringing others to faith. Jesus wants Christians to leave the ninety-nine righteous sheep and seek the one lost sheep until they find it (Luke 15:4–7).

The fifth principle is to build bridges of friendship to communicate the gospel through hospitality. Hospitality is a way of life for the Muslims, and thus, it plays a very important role in opportunities to connect. If a Christian is invited into the home of a Muslim family, he or she will almost always be offered food and drink, no matter how brief the visit is. Friends are treated like family, and traditions in the Muslim family are to share food and deep conversation. There are many examples in the Bible that teach Christians to build a hospitable attitude and practice hospitality. In the Old Testament (Exodus 22:20–22; Leviticus 25:35) it says, "Do not mistreat an alien or oppress him, for you were aliens in Egypt." Abraham, in Genesis 18, welcomed strangers into his tent. In the New Testament, this command to be hospitable occurs throughout its pages: find other examples in Luke 10:5–7; Romans 12:13; Hebrews 13:1–3; 2 Peter1:11; and 3 John 1:1–5. In the tradition of Abraham, Christians should open their homes and churches to non-Christians and be hospitable.

The sixth principle is to understand that God uses the body of Christ (i.e., the church) for his mission (i.e., to share Christ's love and peace with Muslims.) The mission field is at the Christian's doorstep in North America. Mission is meant to cross the political, economical, or cultural boundaries to take the good news of the one-true God to those who have fallen and who are separated from God. The church mission must guard, reveal, and communicate love with the people around it.

The church plays many roles in bringing salvation to the world. It stands as the light of the world (Matthew 5:14). The church should not only send people out into the field but should also attract people to come join the fellowship and hear the good news. Mission has its origin in God. We see God graciously seeking Adam and Eve—who were guilty sinners—and provide for their restoration (Genesis 3, 7:15). God called Adam, "Where are you?" This is similar to the New Testament, when God brought the nations to where the disciples were in Jerusalem. In Acts 2, on the day of Pentecost, the body of Christ was called out to prayer and fellowship. They were all together in one place, and suddenly the Holy Spirit filled that place. The Bible records that many godly men and women from all over the world were gathered in Jerusalem to celebrate Passover. There were more than thirteen nations and languages. I do not believe that all were Jews; they were convicted by the Holy Spirit, accepted the message, and returned to their countries as ambassadors for God. Arabs were part of these ambassadors.

Christians agree that the message of the New Testament entails missions. We call it the Great Commission. The dominated idea of *mission* in most of our churches is to leave our own countries and travel to another country. The church has a mandate to take the gospel message of salvation to the ends of the earth and to make disciples of Christ in every nation. I believe every lay person has the opportunity for sharing the gospel and for being a missionary in his or her church and country. Although it has always been God's plan for the church to go into the world, this strategy is only half of God's equation for reaching the people. Over the centuries, the church has nearly missed part of God's plan, reaching the world that God brings to your community and church.

I keep hearing this statement in our churches: "I am going to the ends of the earth: God called me to leave my job, do fund-raising, sell my house, pack my stuff, and move to another country." I have no problem with the Great Commission. My question is this: What about those strangers (e.g., Muslims) who come to live close to our churches? Who is going to share the gospel with them? Do we need to wait for God to send missionaries or Arab-speaking Christians as missionaries to the United States to share the gospel with them? As the church is mobilized to "go" to Muslim countries, it is entirely possible that we will overlook the fact that the future leaders of the 10/40 window are in our country, communities, and universities. And these leaders are easily reached with the good news about Jesus's cross through friendship and love. The 10/40 window is simply a term used to describe a region of the world within 10 and 40 degrees latitude from Western Africa to Eastern Asia. There are over 3 billion unreached people in the world today. Of those 3.2 billion people, 85% live in or near the 10/40 window. In the 10/40 window there are approximately 775 million Muslims, 800 million Hindus, and 250 million Buddhists. The people who are lost in the 10/40 Window are not "more lost" than your neighbor or family member who does not know Christ. But, they are "unreached" in the sense that they have not had an opportunity to hear the Gospel, and now are our neighbors and in the backyard of the church.

To reach out to the Muslims in the world, we should first minister to those Muslims in North America. We need to pray for the movement of the Holy Spirit and that God will pour his love into our hearts and into the people around us, including Muslims. We need to reach those now who can influence others and those who are arriving each day.

The seventh principle is to seek the kingdom of God first. The biggest issue or priority in a Christian's life should be seeking God first, above all else. Kingdom and righteousness and all these things will be given to you (Matthew 6: 28–33, NIV). It is from seeking the kingdom of God and his righteousness that food, clothing, and shelter are provided and all other life worries are resolved. Life's worries have sent many families into depression and turmoil that seems to last for generations. Muslims are seeking a "kingdom" in this world. The Islamic religion is seeking to reach out to the world to establish an Islamic religion on Earth. Many come to the United States for this reason.

The Quran is very clear that it is man who, through his actions, will earn paradise or fire in the hereafter. Muslims obtain their kingdom by their work, but Christians obtain the kingdom of God by faith (Romans 1: 17; 3:21–31.) Unfortunately, some followers of Jesus are living under the bondage of religion, using the system of the world in the kingdom of God. They end up being religious, bitter, and angry toward God, like Cain. True Christians win eternity and the promised land by faith (Hebrews 11) The signs of religion are fanaticism, division, and lack of understanding (1 Corinthians 1:10–13), as well as quarrels about who is going to be the greatest (John 13:17). But faith brings unity. We, as believers, are called by God to live by faith, and it is the first vision every believer should receive in order to live a victorious life on earth (Hebrews 11; Ephesians 6:10–18). The only way to operate in God's kingdom is by faith and not by anything else. Faith does not work and operate without love (Galatians 5:6) and love always follows faith (1 John 3:23).

The eighth principle is about prayer. I believe there are three approaches to praying for Muslims salvation:

- Be with a group that has united hearts and minds for praying to Muslims. In the book of Acts, the *whole community* interceded (Acts 1:4); they all *joined together* constantly in prayer (Acts 2:1). They were *all together* in one place (Acts 5:12–14 and 12:2). When they heard the power of God was with Peter and John, and they saw Peter and John's courage in spite of threats from the Jewish leaders, who were telling them not to speak or teach at all in the name of Jesus, the disciples raised their *voices together*, praising and praying to God (Acts 4:24–31).
- Be encouraged by God's intervention and let answered prayers lead to more prayers. The early church prayed earnestly and persistently and did not give up (Luke 18:1–8; Matthew 6:5–8). When we see and hear hundreds of Muslims come to faith in Christ through God's revelation, dreams, and visions—without a human messenger—we deeply rejoice and know in our spirits that God is answering our prayers.
- Pray amid persecution and sufferings (i.e., difficult times) for Muslims who accepted Christ. The early church prayed for the father's heart and will because they were suffering and persecuted (Ephesians 5:17). Jesus prayed before the cross. "My Father if it is

possible may this cup be taken from me yet not as I will, but as you will" (Matthew 26:39, NIV).

An important distinction is that Christian prayers are different from Muslim prayers. Prayer is not formatted or obligated in terms of time of day or the number of times required. Christian prayer is simply communicating with or talking to God. The Bible teaches us that prayer is not simply saying words. "And when you pray, do not keep on babbling like pagans, (as people of other religions do) for they think they will be heard because of their many words" (Matthew 6:7, NIV). Christian prayer is effective and can change a person's life. The Bible gives us directions for how to pray. These are crucial concepts to share with Muslims about Christianity.

1. Pray with faith (Matthew 8:13, 9:29; Mark 11:25–26; Hebrews 11:6).
2. Pray with an attitude of forgiveness (Matthew 6:14–15; James 5:14–16).
3. Pray with a pure heart (Isaiah 59:1–2; Psalm 66:18).
4. Pray with your leader and mature people (James 5:14–15).
5. Pray with thanksgiving (Philippians 3:6).
6. Pray continually (1 Thessalonians 5:17–18).
7. Pray with clear motivation (James 4:1–3).
8. Pray with the Holy Spirit, his direction (Matthew 26:41–42; Romans 8:26–28).
9. Pray with humbleness (Luke 18:9–14; 2 Chronicles 7:14).
10. Pray in the name of Jesus (Matthew 28:17–19; Luke 8:44; James 5:13–18).
11. Pray the Word of God (Psalms 119:15, 48; Jeremiah 23:29; Acts 4:23–31).
12. Pray the promises of God (1 King 8; Psalms 34:10; 2 Peter 1:2–4).

God is sending hundreds of Christians to the Islamic mission field overseas. We are under orders. Our Lord Jesus commanded us to go, to preach, and to make disciples. We have no choice. We are ambassadors under authority. God's unchangeable motive is that by preaching the gospel of peace, people will hear, believe, and be saved (Romans 10:9–15, NIV). Dr. Billy Graham said, "We engage in evangelism today not because we like to, or because we choose to, but because we have been told to" (Graham 1989, 14). When Christians consider the situation of Muslims, they could describe them as blind, in darkness, proud of what they believe, but yet under the power of Satan. God called us to be instruments that he will use to open their eyes (Acts 26:18) Muslims are not looking for another religion; they are looking for better life and for freedom. Your Muslim friend will never give up his beliefs and religion if he doesn't experience God's peace.

Chapter 1: The Great Commission

Questions for Reflection:

1. What is *mission*? Where is the mission field? And what a critical message to Muslims?

2. What can you do to feel more comfortable with sharing your faith with a Muslim acquaintance?

3. Who is a lost sheep you want to focus on? Is there someone specific you can pray for?

4. Is there a division in Christ's family? Explain?

5. What is one way to build trust with Muslims?
   o Answer: Acts of love
   o Building trust through hospitality or friendship

6. How do Muslim' believe they will obtain the kingdom of God?
   o Answer: Muslims think it is through their works, but Christians will win the kingdom of God through their faith.

7. What is a major distinction between Christian and Muslim prayer?
    o   Answer: Christian prayer is simply communicating or talking to God. Muslims think they must pray the same words over again at rigid requirements for time and number each day.

CHAPTER 2

WHY IS IT DIFFICULT FOR CHRISTIANS TO EVANGELIZE TO SHI'A MUSLIMS?

It is not an easy task to profess one's beliefs or to share God with another person. There are many, many challenges. Understanding is critical for allowing awareness of the obstacles against American Christians for planting seeds of hope in the hearts of Muslims and non-Muslims in general. The Holy Spirit will then be allowed to do its work. In this chapter, I will attempt to tackle the following questions: Why don't Christians evangelize to Muslims? What are the major restrictions that make both Muslims and Christians uninterested in each other's teachings? In my experience, there are six major obstacles that hinder the delivery of the message of salvation through Jesus.

- Historical
- Spiritual
- Cultural
- Psychological
- Political
- Personal

Unfortunately, there are many restrictions that make it difficult for Christians to be effective in evangelism to the Muslims. In this chapter,

I will answer the following question: Why don't Christians evangelize Muslims? Stated another way, why do Muslims prefer to be distant from Christians? What are the major restrictions that make both Muslims and Christians uninterested in each other's teachings? I shared six areas where Christians and Muslims face obstacles. Each obstacle has multiple facets that I pray will improve understanding and pave the way for understanding and removal of these obstacles.

Historical Obstacles

Historically, there are negative factors that have damaged the relationships between Christians and Muslims. These negative factors cause grave misunderstandings about Christ's love and redemption, blinding Muslims' eyes toward the truth about Christ and Christianity. The Muslims' history has been both rich and troubling. Islam is rich in culture, art, and literature but troubling in politics and religion.

One historical factor negatively affecting evangelism is Christians' prejudice toward Muslims and vice versa. Both Christians and Muslims are proud of their own heritages and look down upon others who don't have the same beliefs. However, Christians must recognize that the word of God is the authority. Paul warned the Christians in Corinth about pride; we know that we all have knowledge. "Knowledge puffs up, while love builds up" (1 Corinthians 8:1, NIV). Islam has not emerged out of the blue. Some have said, "if Christians were sharing the truth of Jesus's love faithfully, there would not be Islam today."

Another historical factor negatively affecting evangelism is the predominance of strict regulations and violence on the part of Islam and Christianity alike. If we want to understand the Muslims' thoughts, we need to be aware of the historical developments in the Jewish and Christian settlements and of their teachings on the Arabian Peninsula during the first six centuries. Christian were divided and fought over the Christian doctrine, so we shouldn't be surprised that the result of this was another new teaching and religion. Muhammad preached a new teaching and mandated that Christians change their religion and beliefs in the trinity, the divinity of Christ, and the crucifixion. Christians were to be killed, persecuted, and forced to pay taxes, or they had to leave the Muslim territory. After Muhammad's death in 632 AD, this attitude toward

Christianity continued. During the Umayyah and Abbasid's Caliphate, Muslims continued to invade Christian tribes, villages, and countries. After several campaigns, most Christian tribes in the whole region of Iraq, Syria, Lebanon, Palestine, Egypt, and North Africa were forced to become Muslims and to follow the teaching of Islam.

Many Middle Eastern Christians tolerated the Muslim persecutions and believed that God would bring justice. Western Christians formed armies to seek revenge and to take back the Holy City, Jerusalem, from Muslims, through power and human efforts. The purpose of the Crusades in the eleventh, twelfth, and thirteenth centuries was to invade the Middle East, to help Arab Christians, and to free Jerusalem from Muslim oppression. They believed that no Muslim could ever possess the Holy Land. The pope and religious Christian leaders offered all loyal warriors who fought for Jerusalem a full redemption from their sins. This, of course, caused much enthusiasm in Europe, which led to a succession of crusades. This invasion of the Middle East increased the amount of hate, division, and distrust between the West and the East and, more overly, between native Christians and Arab Muslims. The crusaders committed horrible acts against Jews, Muslims, and even Eastern Christians (atrocities, raping, murdering, and plundering, to name a few). Jews fled to a synagogue and Muslims to a mosque. Crusaders burned the synagogues, killing thousands of Jews and tens of thousands of Muslims. They left a legacy of fear and contempt in the Muslim world. The violence continued during the Ayyubids and Mamluk periods (1127–1516); Muslims determined to fight the crusaders. In the end, it was not the crusaders who suffered the most, but the Middle Eastern Christians and missionaries—who supported the crusaders—who bore the brunt of the punishment of the Crusades.

Other historical factors have emerged throughout history, including Zionism and Muslim nationalism. Zionism was a reaction to the anti-Semitic movement that blamed Jews for every problem in the social order. It is the Jewish nationalist movement that was founded in 1897 in Basel, Switzerland, by Theodor Herzl, and that created the State of Israel in 1948. Political anti-Semitism, which is distinct from religious anti-Judaism characteristics of Christianity, and which culminated in the Holocaust with the murder of nearly six million European Jews.

The American Christian Zionism agenda was to use the US's military power and ancient biblical prophecies in combination to carry out their agenda. Conservative Christians were persuaded to support the Jewish people's desire to return to their ancient homeland in Israel. Ironically, this movement has led to Christian missionaries being killed and persecuted in the Middle East. It has also widened the gap between Christians and Muslims and blocked the message of the cross and peace in the Middle East. When the West formed a resolution to establish an Israeli state, millions of Palestinians became refugees. This led to war in 1948. The war was called the War of Independence, or the War of Liberation by the Israelis. For Palestinians, this war marked the beginning of the events referred to as the Catastrophe or "*al-nakba* النكبه" in Arabic. It was followed by many wars between the Arab countries and Israel in the Middle East: the six-day war between Israel and Arabs in 1967; the War of Attrition in 1970; and the Yom Kippur War in 1973. The West, specifically the United States and Europe, supported these wars. Muslims consider western countries synonymous with Christianity. According to the Arab Muslim world, Christians and Jews are generally regarded as unbelievers rather than "people of the book" (i.e., believers); and they are partners against Islam and the Arab Muslim world. This has caused continual bitterness and hatred by the Muslims in the region against Israel and the Christians. These wars created a huge obstacle gab for missions and evangelism to the Muslims.

Like Zionism, the advent of religious nationalism in the Arab-Muslim world resulted in the Islamic fundamentalist uprising. Nationalist movements arose when the Ottomans sought to westernize their army and administration, similar to what Arab-Christians did in the Middle East. Christian and Muslim students were sent to the West to study the latest in medicine and military technology, but they returned with other knowledge as well. Students learned about patriotism and nationalism, which emphases the ideas of one's homeland, nationality, and native language as essential features of political organization.

Many Muslim clerics and thinkers have regarded nationalism as a divisive Christian western ideology undermining Islamic unity and promoting secularism. These Muslims claim that Islam is the solution since their Islamic national governments imitated the western Christian civilization. They accused their Islamic rulers of having failed to feed the poor and to keep the Muslim identity. Many Muslims founded revivalist Islamic parties to free the world from Christian civilizations and Zionists, and to bring back their meaningful identities as Muslims, true Muslims, and followers of Muhammad.

The fifth historical factor negatively affecting evangelism is the rise of radical Muslim groups in the twentieth century, like the Brethren in Egypt and the Iranian revolution. They were a reaction against the modernism and nationalism, and western civilization has increased the hate of Muslims against Christians and made the task of evangelizing Muslims more difficult.

The radical Shi'a believe that reform must come primarily from lay religious intellectuals rather than from traditional religious leaders. Khomeini was such a man. He was trained at an Islamic seminary in Qum and then became an instructor there, believing that both monarchs were determining to break the power of the 'ulamah (العلماء) and wanted to secularize Iranian society. Khomeini was arrested for publicly accusing the Shah and was exiled to Turkey in 1964. During this time, fundamentalist Iranian Muslims did not express their beliefs. They were in tremendous fear of the government. They followed the Al-Takiyah (التقية) method, which requires believers to hide their faith: "inside, I hate you, but outside I pretend to be your friend." Al-Takiya also meant that the Muslims behaved in a way that pleased the government, not according to their beliefs.

During his exile, Ayatollah Khomeini continued to speak out against the Shah and his government. His lectures and sermons were leading and brainwashing millions of Shi'a people from a distance through taped recordings that were smuggled into Iran. He shared his beliefs, dreams, and plans for the Islamic country. Ayatollah sent a message to Shi'a Muslims in the world: "No one can defeat a nation that receives Allah's orders and obeys them." And the Khomeini said, "Most persistent charges were that the shah was selling Iran to foreign [lands], especially the US, interests [sic] and that this was tantamount to the destruction of Iran's Islamic identity."

During the ten days of Muharram in December 1979, an estimated two million people filled the streets of Azadi Square (then Shahyad Square) in Tehran, the capital city of Iran, to protest the king Shah. Muharam is the customary period of ritual mourning for the death of Imam Husain, but it was used on this occasion to place the antiregime protests firmly within a religious framework. Shi'a marched and waved banners denouncing the Shah and his US ally and demanded the return of Khomeini.

Khomeini issued a proclamation stating that any government appointed by the Shah was illegal and that to serve it was to betray Iran. An estimated seven hundred protesters were killed. On January 16, 1979, Muhammad Reza Shah left Iran and died a year later as an exile in Egypt.

On February 1 of the same year, Ayatollah Khomeini returned to Iran from France. He bowed twice outside the aircraft before the flight to Tehran and thanked Allah. Millions of people received him at his arrival at Tehran's airport. The city was shaken by the sound of them shouting, "God is great" (*Allah o Akbar* الله اكبر). Now there was no more fear or hiding their beliefs from the government and from the world. Syria and the Soviet Union were the first two states to grant recognition to the new government. In November of the same year, in a gesture of defiance toward the United States, labeled "the Great Satan" by Khomeini, the revolutionary guards surrounded the American embassies in Tehran and held its occupants hostage for 444 days.

This Islamic revolution movement led thousands of Arab Shi'a Muslims to shout against their government in the Arab world of Egypt, Syria, Iraq, Bahrain, and Lebanon, and also against the Christian governments in the world. They declared that the Islamic Shi'a should take over their governments like it had in Iran. The fundamentalist clergy, led by Khomeini, cleared away the opposition and established an Islamic republic called "Guardianship of the Islamic Jurists" (*Willayat al-Faqih-* ولاية الفقيه). This religious revival in Iran has touched not only Iran but all parts of the Arab Shi'a Muslim world, and the Khomeini has reminded the Shi'ites of their history of martyrdom. Hezbollah, the Lebanese Arab radical Shi'a, is based on the Shi'a tradition of Islam, specifically in the concept of *Willayat Al-Faqih*, the right to rule. Hezbollah seeks to set up an Islamic government in Lebanon that's modeled after the one in Iran. Hezbollah is dedicated to liberating Jerusalem and eliminating Israel and has formally advocated the ultimate establishment of Islamic Shi'a rule in Lebanon. It is strongly anti-Western, anti-Christian, and anti-Israeli. These fundamentalists Shi'a regard themselves as faithful Muslims. They believe that Islam is not just a religion; it is also an ideology with a political agenda. They control many top political positions.

The sixth historical factor is the pressure of the Islamic fundamentalist teachings. The radical Shi'a Muslims apply the Khomeini's teachings and beliefs; I summarize them below in a few points:

1. The Khomeini's ideologies are that the Islamic state is modeled on the Quran and the community of the prophet could realistically be created and that the men of religion, because of their knowledge of Islamic law, should manage the affairs of the state.

2. Adherence to full Islamic rules is not possible until there is an Islamic government.

3. Who will take the responsibility of leading and guiding the Islamic Shi'a government or the Islamic community (*Ummah*- امة) today? To the Khomeini, the answer to this question lies in the rule of just, pious, and honorable jurists. Today, at the top of Iran's power structure, is the supreme leader, Ayatollah Ali Khamenei, who succeeded Ayatollah Ruhollah Khomeini, the father of the Iranian Revolution, upon Khomeini's death in 1989. According to Iran's constitution, the supreme leader is responsible for the delineation and supervision of "the general policies of the Islamic republic of Iran."

4. The supreme leader rules with dictatorship. Following the ideology of absolute Wilayat al-Faqih، ولاية الفقيه establish Islamic Shi'a government (governance of the jurist). This meant that the party's "leadership, direction, mandate, decisions of war and peace, and so on, is in the hand of the supreme Shi'a leader" "Wali al-Faqih."

5. The supreme leader did not fulfill his prerevolution promises to the Shi'a people, but instead, they marginalized and crashed the opposition groups like Christians and those who opposed the clerical rules. If you angered Khomeini, chances were that you would die.

6. The Islamic religion has rules for every walk of life. There are laws for economic, social, civil, and spiritual affairs.

7. The supreme leader ordered the establishment of many institutions to merge power and to safeguard the cleric leadership. Many people

were laid off, and lots of books were revised or burnt according to the new Islamic values.

8. A newly established Islamic judiciary system sentenced many Christian Iranians to death and long-term imprisonment. Anyone in opposition to those radical changes was sentenced to death. Cleveland said, "Islamization occurred in the realm of officially approved social behavior. A dress required all women, including female civil servants, to wear the loose fitting garments and headscarf known as hijab was introduced in 1980. The regime further sought to purify society in implementing measures that ranged from banning music and dancing in public places to cracking down on drug dealers to razing Tahran's red light district" (Cleveland 2000, 423).

9. The destruction of the state of Israel, which is a central ideological tenet of the Shi'a radical Muslims. Islamic Iranian regime was shown on the Iranian Television and other international networks like CNN on September 22, 2003, with things like "Israel must be uprooted and erased from history" inscribed on three ballistic Shahab missiles in a military parade in Teheran. According to the ideology of the Shi'a Islamic clerics ruling Iran, Judaism is considered a religion, but the Jews are not considered a nation and, therefore, there is no place for a Jewish state and certainly not on Muslim lands or in Jerusalem, which is a holy city to all Muslims.

10. The final teaching is the Holocaust denial. according to the leaders of the Islamic regime in Iran, the Jews make use of the enormity of the Holocaust to fool the world and to hide their real aims.

11. Post-revolutionary Iran sees itself as the champion of the Shi'a Muslims in the Middle East. Iran's strategic goal is to appear as the dominant power in the Middle East, and eventually, the entire Islamic world. It seeks to move back US influence in the Middle East and to work towards Israel's destruction. The Middle East is currently in the midst of widespread instability, civil war and suffering. Syria, Iraq, Lebanon, Bahrain, the West Bank and Gaza Strip, Tunisia, Libya, Turkey, Egypt, and Yemen have all experienced major instability over the last two-decade.

Hezbollah, a Shi'a Islamist political party viewed as a terrorist organization by United Stated and many European countries, has committed hundreds of terrorist attacks around the world. It attacks always in harmony with the agenda of its supporter – Iran. Hezbollah is an Arabic name made up of two words, Hezb-Allah, which means "Party of God". Hezbollah was established by the Revolutionary Guards in Iran in the early 1980s during the civil war in Lebanon. Throughout the 1980s, Hezbollah engaged in increasingly complex attacks against Israel and fought in Lebanon's Civil War (1975–90). During that time, Hezbollah engaged in terrorist attacks directed mainly against Israel, the Christian militia and Westerners. Since 1990, Hezbollah has been the only non-governmental organization permitted to maintain an armed wing for Iran in Lebanon and entire Middle East. Hezbollah launched a sustained guerrilla campaign against Israel in southern Lebanon until Israel's withdrawal in 2000. And in 2006, Hezbollah initiated a war on Israel without seeking the consent of the Lebanese official government.

As a Lebanese involved with the Christian militia in South Lebanon, my experience with Hezbollah turned my life upside down. In 1985, I joined the Lebanese Army to fight Hezbollah and defend my beloved people from the new radical Muslim ideologies. During one of my military missions in Lebanon, I stood on a landmine that was planted by the militia of Hezbollah. The landmine exploded right under my feet, and I was suddenly dying on the ground. I was terrified. I tried to hold my breath inside of me, thinking that my spirit was about to come out of me. I started to pray and shouted with all my strength, "Jesus, forgive my sins and save me. I don't want to go to hell. If you save me and keep me alive, I will follow you." As soon as I finished my prayer, I heard a voice like a wind coming from heaven. It came upon me, and I felt peaceful. I looked at my body, covered with blood, and I saw my left leg completely burned and hanging on the skin. My leg is gone, but I am still alive! It was a tragic event, but God saved me and turned it for good, hope and life. He changed my life forever. You can read my whole story in my first book, "The Good Soldier: Running on The Road of Hope."

Today, Hezbollah is still playing a vital role in the Syrian Civil War and continues to support pro-Iranian Shi'a groups in Iraq, Yemen, Bahrain, and the Palestinian territories. Hezbollah's political culture has never been democratic. It is based on the "Principle of the Guardianship of the Islamic Jurist" (Walayat Faqih). In general, it can be said that since its establishment Hezbollah has aspired to establish an Islamic republic in Lebanon and the Middle East based on the Iranian model, which is very far from being a model of liberal democracy.

On May 6, 2018, Lebanon held its first legislative election since 2009, and Hezbollah received a majority of seats, making it politically dominant with control of the Lebanese parliament, Lebanese military, economy and security.

Hezbollah added new aims:

1. Defend the Shi'a communities and allies in the region.
2. Fight the takfiris; "تكفيريين" ", the Sunni Islamists. Hezbollah has acted as one of the most effective fighting forces against the Islamic State group (ISIS).
3. Protect the Assad regime, which is a strategic interest for Hezbollah and its supporter, Iran. Hezbollah's involvement in Syria has increased to the level of approximately 5,000 or more fighters.

Currently, the United Nations, the United States and the International Cooperation are trying to reduce Hezbollah's power, military capability, and influence. Their goals are to expand the circle of countries that view Hezbollah as a terrorist organization, reduce the possibility of military and financial assistance that Hezbollah receives, and wage an international campaign to freeze or reduce the organization's sources of income.

12. Radical Sunni Muslims like: Al-Akhwan al-Muslimene, ISIS, and Al-Anssar, Hammas, Al-Qaida and many other Islamic sects adopted Iran's supreme leaders' ideologies and had terror attacks with fatalities on US soil. Some examples follow in the list below.
    - September 11, 2001: Nineteen radical Muslims, al Qaeda members, hijacked four US passenger airliners. Two were flown into the twin towers in New York; one crashed into

the Pentagon; and another crashed into the Pennsylvania countryside after passengers attempted to wrest control of the aircraft to prevent an attack on the US Capitol. At the World Trade Center site 2,753 people were killed; 184 at the Pentagon; and 40 in Shanksville, Pennsylvania. A total of 2,977 people were killed.

- April 15, 2013: Twin bomb blasts exploded near the finish line of the Boston Marathon, killing three and wounding at least 264. This attack was carried out by two Muslims, Tamerlan Tsarnaev and Dzhokhar Tsarnaev.

- July 16, 2015: Mohammad Abdulazeez opened fire on a military recruiting center and a navy reserve facility in Chattanooga, Tennessee, killing four US Marines and one navy sailor.

- December 2, 2015: Married couple Syed Rizwan Farook and Tashfeen Malik opened fire on a holiday party that was taking place at the Inland Regional Center in San Bernardino, California, killing fourteen people.

- June 12, 2016: Omar Mateen, an American man who'd pledged allegiance to ISIS ideology, killed forty-nine people and wounded others in a shooting spree at a gay nightclub in Orlando.

- October 31, 2017: Eight people were killed and almost a dozen were injured by saifullah Habbullaevic Saipov in a rented pickup truck driven down a busy bicycle path in New York. Authorities claimed the attack was made in the name of ISIS.

- In 2019: The war in the Middle East and the instability in the world increased, caused by radical Muslims ideologies. Muslim immigration continues to the West and to the US more than ever.

Spiritual Obstacles

The reality of being Muslim in the Muslim world is far more complex than these historical events. Most Muslims who come to the North America are strongly bound by the influence of spiritual and magical Islamic teachings. Most immigrant Muslims in North America carry the scars of a defective relationship with their religion from back home. Generally, transplanted Muslims prefer to be distant from Christians and intentionally live far away from other ethnic groups.

Muslims have been deceived by false leaders and teachers about magic and witchcraft that have created a powerful spiritual obstacle. There is a prevalence of disturbing stories about Spirits in the Muslim countries. Folk Muslims confess Allah but worship spirits and are more concerned with magic than with Muhammad because folk Islam blends animism with Islam. Just as western Evangelical Christians grieve over the materialism that negatively impacts Christianity, so do radical Muslims grieve over magic practices infiltrating Islam.

Many Muslims utilize Islamic leaders who specialize in magic. It is common for leader sheikhs, or clergies, to write verses from the Quran to help a businessperson have a successful business trip; or, if a young man wants to influence a girl to love him, he asks someone to hide pieces of written texts under her mattress. Similar customs are also practiced by a family that wants to have a baby. One can also find different forms of sorcery—known as white magic or black magic—whose aims are only to influence others, not to kill or harm them. Black magic also occurs in the Muslim world, through which people try to destroy others. The love of money is a big motive for using magic. These manifestations are usually not limited to Islam, but they occur and show the sadness and desperation in Muslim people over the culture's failure to provide them with real comfort or satisfactory answers to the difficulties and problems in their lives.

A foremost spiritual obstacle is the clash of ideologies and lack of unity among Christians. Muslims see this lack of agreement rather than Christ's love among Christian scholars and theologians as a reason not to believe Christ's message. Who is right and who is wrong? This dispute and division between Christians does not reflect a good picture of Christ or Christianity among Muslims.

Christians often focus on the church inwardly instead of outwardly. They are busy solving their doctrinal issues, condemning others, and fighting over positions instead of focusing on the mission field. Christians make a lot of worldly excuses that prevent their involvement in the Muslim field or in any ministry relating to Muslims.

Islam's perception of ancient Christianity was polytheism, consisting of idol worship reverenced in the temple of Ka'ba (كعبة). Muslims perceive that the Christians of today are fanatically putting the saints above Jesus Christ. They think that, to worship them, Christians build idols of saints in and outside of their homes. Icons and pictures fill their houses for protection. Church priests ask their followers to pray to these icons and ask them to redeem them and to protect them from war. They employ saints as mediators between themselves and Christ. For example, they pray, "Mary, mother of God, our redeemer, ask your son, Jesus, to forgive our sins." Muslims look at these acts of Christians as paganism.

Christians often have primitive, if not nonexistent, knowledge of Islam and its rituals. Christians do not recognize that there are different sects, theologies, philosophies, and mystical doctrines among Muslims. In order to gain respect and credibility, it is essential for Christians to be well-informed about Islam. Tragically, many Christians in the West have severely misunderstood and underestimated Islam. The Muslim mind encompasses many channels and a tapestry of differing views on important issues—a mosaic of distinctive differences.

As previously suggested, Christians often have a prejudice against Muslims. For example, in the case when Muslims do believe in Christ, Christians tend to eye them critically, distrust them, and distance themselves. Christians think that they are spies or that they are looking for a cheap education in a Christian school. They may have ulterior motives of "stealing" the heart of a nice girl from their "flock" or one of the few jobs available! Thus, they are not accepted as a fellow Christians, which—if they were—would allow for more faith growth and discipleship among other Muslims.

Likely the most important spiritual obstacle is combating the work of the spirit of the Antichrist. We are living in a time when the battle between the kingdom of God and the kingdom of Satan is heating up as never before. When we say *antichrist*, that means *anti-Messiah*. Anti- is a Greek preposition. It has two meanings, and both apply. First, it means *against*. So the first operation is against Christ. The second meaning is *in place of*. The ultimate purpose is to put a false Christ in place of the true Christ. The biblical scripture in 1 John 4:1–3, NIV, states, "Dear friends, do not believe every spirit, but test the spirits to see whether they are from

God, because many false prophets have gone out into the world. This is how you can recognize the Spirit of God: Every spirit that acknowledges that Jesus Christ has come in the flesh is from God, but every spirit that does not acknowledge Jesus is not from God. This is the spirit of the antichrist, which you have heard is coming and even now is already in the world." And in 1 John 4:14–15, NIV, it states, "And we have seen and testify that the Father has sent his Son to be the Savior of the world. If anyone acknowledges that Jesus is the Son of God, God lives in them and they in God."

Islam absolutely denies that Jesus is the Son of God. You can talk to Muslims about Jesus as a prophet, and they will give you careful attention. In fact, the Quran acknowledges Jesus as a prophet, a savior, and even as a Messiah. But when you say he is the Son of God, you bring out the most intense, bitter opposition. In the famous mosque in Jerusalem that is called the Dome of the Rock, which is built on the site of what was once the Temple of Solomon, the Arabic inscriptions around it say, "God has no need of a son" twice. Islam denies certain fundamentals of the Christian faith, like the atoning death of Jesus on the cross. Mohammad taught that Jesus did not die and that there is no atonement and, because there is no atonement, there is no forgiveness. Thus, no Muslim has the assurance of sins forgiven at any time. Therefore, according to scripture (1 John 4:1–3, 14–15, NIV), we conclude the teachings of Mohammad and Islam is antichrist.

Cultural Obstacles

A problem that deserves careful attention is the indivisible bond between culture, identity, and religion. At the heart of the difficulty with reaching Muslim hearts for Christ is a series of stereotypical beliefs in Christian thinking, many of which arise from prejudice and cultural misunderstanding. Christians look at Muslims in stereotypical terms, as a homogeneous group marked by religious zeal, violent methods, and radical acts—all of which are aggressive to the United States. This oversimplified picture is based on the sensational manifestations of Muslim assertion, which reached its peak in the decade following the Iranian revolution. After the September 11 attacks, many Christians made assumptions about Muslims based on their appearances or their accents, sometimes showing them little or no respect. Some even considered them to be from a third-class country or assumed that they belonged to violent groups. These assumptions create a feeling of superiority in Christians and caused a retreat from interacting with Muslims around them, which led to covering up this problem with isolation.

Christians often fail in contextualization of Christianity's message. Witnessing to Muslims requires an understanding of the worldview of the Muslim culture. For change to occur, the gospel must speak to their deep core beliefs and answer the questions that people are asking. Change is the goal of sharing the message. Good contextualization demands that the evangelist understand his or her own worldview before beginning to transmit his or her message. The goal is that the gospel of Jesus Christ is communicated to transform Muslim beliefs.

An obvious and major cultural obstacle is that Christians have a limited knowledge of the language of Muslims. Many speak English as a second language, but their native language is of the country where they live. It can be Arabic, Farsi, Lebanese, Urdu, or Indonesian. Christians can make huge strides in building relationship by learning simple phases in a Muslim's native language. For example, knowing that *aloha* means *hello* in Hawaiian—language is a bridge to opening conversation. You will gain someone's attention, and likely a warm smile, if you speak in his or her beloved language. Simple things, like saying hello or *As-salāmu 'Alaykum* (in Arabic, السلام عليكم, Arabic pronunciation: [as-salamu 'Alaykum]) is a greeting in Arabic that means *Peace be upon you*.

Another cultural difference that can create misunderstanding is the concept of time. Muslims are people-oriented or community-oriented and have little interest in specific or exact designations of time. This contrasts with Western culture. For example, where a westerner says, "I will come and visit you tomorrow at six o'clock in the evening," a Muslim would say, "I will come to see you tomorrow evening." The evening may mean anytime between three o'clock and six or eight at night. Muslims must manage their time in a different way than they are accustomed to in order to be punctual for appointments or classes.

Culture makes it difficult for Christians to develop genuine friendships with Shi'a Muslims. Shi'a Muslim people live in a community where everyone personally knows all the other people living in the neighborhood.

They visit each other daily and even share meals together. Middle Easterners don't find this attitude when they meet Christians. Neighborhoods in the United States have grown distant. People living in apartments or subdivisions rarely know the names of their neighbors, much less have a friendship with them. This is very different from Shi'a rich customs.

When a Shi'a comes to North America from places where no Christian witness or Bible teaching has been permitted for centuries, he or she encounters many challenges. On one hand, he or she wants to obey the Islamic laws and not lose his or her identity, but on the other hand, there is pressure from the North American society and culture. People in this situation become different, religiously. They behave differently and, to protect themselves, may pretend that they do not follow Islam. This can open them to being liberal in their thinking. They are torn by their attraction to the old Islamic life, fashion, and teaching. They also desire to fit in and to accept the ways of their new homes in North America. In one sense, it is true to say that the Islamic teachings and laws hold their worldviews together. At the same time, it is also true to say that North American culture has influenced their worldviews and customs. Internally, they struggle with their own Islamic teachings. The first few years after they arrive in the North America are the hardest for Shi'a Muslims. When they accommodate to North American culture, they are in opposition to the core of their Islamic teachings. Many suffer from loneliness, poverty, unfamiliarity with English, and the absence of extended family and fellow Muslims who share their faith. They value their cultural heritage and do not wish to lose it. Gradually, as they stay longer, they realize that returning home is no longer a viable possibility. They cannot practice their faith as they ought to, and they begin to settle into North American culture and context. This issue increases the feeling of homesickness. Most of them bring their spouses and family members with them, and often spouses have a tremendous need for friendship. They feel isolated by idleness, language barriers, and joblessness. They miss their families, friends, and neighbors more than ever. They feel that no one cares for them, and they become lonelier and unsure of themselves, even inferior to their American counterparts.

Shi'a Muslims struggle with three fundamental questions: Can the Shi'a law be changed? Can the Shi'as' teachings be updated? And can the teachings be supplemented? This dynamic interaction between classical law and human culture continues today. They struggle with whether it is possible to join in "*Khutba-* خطبة" service on Sunday instead of Friday, since that is the only day they are free from work. The classical Shi'a says no, but many moderate Muslims say yes, since the primary duty is the worship of God. In fact, many mosques in North America now conduct worship on Sundays.

The Shi'a family structure and customs in North America are also challenged and are in stark contrast to those in North America. One of the most important areas in the Islamic faith is family ties and bonds. Living in North America, these family ties are threatened. Fathers or husbands in the Muslim Countries mostly dominate the family. It is hard for the modern women's movement in North American countries to change this determination because it is written in the Quran that man is stronger than a woman (Sura al-Nisa' 4:34; also in Sura al-baqara 2:282). It says, "men are more intelligent than women are, and two Muslim women equals that of one Muslim man in legal cases." Abd al-Massih writes, "Men are richer, since they pay the bridal dowry, and in Paradise there live far more men than women because men fear Allah more and fight for him with weapons!" (Abd al-Massih 2003, 4). Women generally do the domestic work of the house; this is required of them by Islam. The Shi'a selects his marriage partner differently than westerners. There is little contact between young men and young women in most parts of the Arab world. The selection of a marriage partner is generally organized by parents and, in many occasions, it is solely the parents' decision. All wives shall be believing Muslims, devoted to Allah and Muhammad, and obedient to their husbands. Muhammad did not care much about whether they were still virgins or already married! However, he determined that they should spend little money and live modestly (al Ahzab 33:28, 33:31, 33:33; al-Thrim 66:5).

Ultimately, the young Shi'a marries—one way or another. Young men who could not find Shi'a partners import their brides from their home countries or, in some cases, marry outside the faith. Shi'a marriage is not a sacrament, but rather, it is a legal, binding contract between a man and woman. A significant number of young, second- and third-generation Shi'a Muslims leave their faith in North America. They have lost their Islamic sense of direction in life. They begin to move beyond class restrictions to start their own businesses, often relying on traditional skills to begin restaurants, coffeehouses, bakeries, and grocery stores.

When Shi'a Muslims begin to eat or drink, they end their meal with brief words of praise and thanksgiving to God "*bismillah al-rahman al-raheem-* الرحيم. بسم الله الرحمان الرحيم" This means, "in the name of Allah, the Merciful, the compassionate." Some Shi'a Muslims regard wasting food as a sin. Some types of food are permitted, and some are prohibited. All food and drinks are allowed except the following, which are prohibited in the Quran: 1.) Pork and its by-products in any form, 2.) The flesh of animals that have died without being slaughtered or bled fully, 3.) The manner of slaughtering an animal prescribed by Islam is to slit its throat in a swift and merciful manner, saying, *bismillah, Allahu Akbar* (in the name of God, God is greater.), and 4.) Any food over which the name of a deity other than God has been invoked and the meat of any animal slaughtered in the name of anyone other than God.

Many Shi'a Muslims break these prohibitions regarding food. They enter Christian homes and eat whatever is offered to them even without asking about it.

In North America, Shi'a Muslims do not observe their holidays as they did in their own countries. Shi'a Muslim holidays and festivals lose their value in the life of a North American Shi'a Muslim. Complicating matters is the fact that the Shi'a Muslim calendar is lunar and moves eleven days earlier each year, in contrast with the Western solar calendar. Families and relatives celebrate festivals by meeting to share a meal and to give gifts to children. Coordinating days off at work and at school make observing these festivals difficult or even impossible in North America. Muslim fundamentalists have caused women to live in hardship by imposing more religious and ethical rules on them. They justify these impositions by saying that women are weak and poor-spirited. The Shi'a Muslim woman's views toward the West are complex. Women feel that they are spiritually equal to men, but inequalities are accepted in terms of differing roles in society. Shi'a women in North America are mostly educated and, as the Muslim American Pew Research Center notes that "69 percent believe that women are treated equally well and 23 percent believe that Islam treats men better than women," wearing the veil "*Hijab*, حجاب or *purdah*" is prescribed to women by a direct order from the Quran. Hijabs protect a woman's dignity and honor but also counteract her sexuality so that she can be a positive, constructive force in society rather than a harmful one.

Religion teaches Shi'a women to be sensitive in the presence of the opposite sex and in the presence of strangers. This is called a sense of "*Haya-* حيه" that means *shyness*. Women feel intense shame and tremendous fear of losing the honor of their families when they expose their faces. In the United States, newly arrived Arab Shi'a Muslims are often deeply shocked by the open lack of shame. Faith, to them, is a guiding force that drives every thought or action in both private and public life because faith is a measure by which every Shi'a Muslim is judged in the afterlife. Delong-Bas says, "They define belief (Iman- ايمان) an attitude that grow out of absolute trust and confidence (tawakkul- توكل) in God. Tawakkul is both religious duty and a condition of faith. Faith should lead to both individual piety and the pursuit of good works."

Shi'a Muslims arrive in North America with certain stereotypical views: all North Americans are Christians; all Christians are ignorant, misinformed, hard to understand, independent, materialistic, and have no moral standards. They also think that Islam is the universal religion and the preeminent world power. Unquestionably, they believe Islam is the only way to heaven. Shi'a Muslims, therefore, are compelled to maintain a separate Islamic subculture. After September 11, 2001, these strong beliefs contributed to persecution and suffering. Most Muslim Americans are made to feel ashamed of their ancestors and of their former homeland. As a result, some have avoided reference to their Muslim heritage—for instance, often describing themselves in terms of the geographic regions and heritages from which they came or to which they belong. Also, to assimilate completely into North American society, some have changed their names to ones that sound more American (e.g., *Mohammad* to *Mo*).

Psychological Obstacles

Christians often don't understand Muslims' psychological makeup. Muslims are generally multidimensional, multilinguistic, multicultural people with a broad view and deep existential experience; therefore, their psychological struggles also reflect that combination of conditions, dynamics, and world views. Complex factors can lead to the need for psychological counseling.

Muslim people normally do not seek psychological treatment options readily unless their situations become absolutely critical. Dr. Naji Abi-Hashem is a clinical and cultural psychologist and author, who indicates in his articles Arab Americans: Understanding Their Challenges, Needs, and Struggles that the following stress-related symptoms are common among Muslims, including: "being on edge, highly nervous, easily scared, feeling caged, venting anger, feeling crippled or immobilized, becoming pushy and irritable, quickly losing their temper in public, e.g., yelling, shouting, complaining, cursing in public and even ladies do this now, which represents totally a new phenomenon. With the increase of the stressful events, economic hardship and extremely high inflation, political uncertainties, and ongoing conflicts, and the decrease of material resources and monthly income, many people have become tight with their money and very self-protective. Some have become even dishonest and manipulative in order to gain more."

It is helpful to consider the complexity of the psychological factors to help understand Muslims yet also remember to rely on the Holy Spirit to sort through such obstacles and encourage them to open their hearts to Christ's love.

Political Obstacles

The political tension in the world is growing between Christians and Muslims and among Muslims themselves. Politics, not theology, was at the root of the Christian and Muslim split to start with. Muslims' perceptions are that the political problem is the United States' policy toward the Israeli-Palestinian conflict and toward Iraq. Most Muslims view US policies toward the Muslim world very negatively. The terrorist attacks on the United States continue to cast a long shadow over Muslim Americans. Most Muslims say that, since the September 11 attacks, it is difficult to be a Muslim in the United States.

Too often in Muslim countries, the media portrays the West—and particularly, the United States—as a country filled with Christian "crusaders," but also as a dangerous place to live, full of adulterers and thieves. When Muslims come here, they have many fears. It is overwhelming to them, especially if they are living alone. They cannot trust people the way they did in their own countries. Muslim media propagates their ideologies and attacks Christian teachings.

Hezbollah—also transliterated as *Hizbullah* or *Hizballah*—is a Shi'a Islamist militant group and political party based in Lebanon. It has its own internet website, as well as one for the Islamic resistance. Hezbollah operates a satellite television station from Lebanon, *Al-Manar* TV, or *the Lighthouse,* as well as a radio station, *al-Nour,* which means *the light.* Qubth Ut Alla قبضة الله, *the Fist of God,* is the monthly magazine of Hezbollah's paramilitary wing. Al Manar broadcasts news in Arabic, English, French, and Hebrew, and is widely watched both in Lebanon and in other Arab countries. Its transmission in France (even via satellite, not by any station based on French territory) is controversial. It is also broadcast in Hebrew as part of its psychological warfare against Israel. It has been accused of promoting religious and racial hatred against Christians and Jews, which is a criminal offense in France and the US. The radical Shi'a conceives of the western media as a powerful and oppressive weapon in the hands of the enemy, through which the Israeli depicts him- or herself as an innocent and oppressed survivor of the Nazi era. The radical Shi'a also views the media as an instrument used by the West to propagate its culture throughout the world. Although this view applies to the western media generally, it relates to the US media specifically. Shi'a wish to advance the cause of their ideals; however, they view US media negatively.

Personal Obstacles

Christians should take care when being sent out to evangelize to Muslims. Improperly prepared and insufficiently grounded with a personal relationship with Christ, they may cause more damage than good. Material comforts, superiorities, prejudices, complacency, superficial repentance, and little faith of sharing the gospel are major obstacles that can be overcome only by acknowledgement and confession of Christians' own sins. It is imperative to leave our priorities behind and to follow Jesus's steps and be filled with his love and power in order to overcome the obstacles they can face in reaching out to Muslims.

Likely, one major personal obstacles is a fear of failure. What if, as a result of my evangelizing, a Muslim does not come to know Christ? No one likes to feel like he or she is a failure. It is important to remember our responsibility in evangelism: it is to plant a seed. Therefore, if we have told someone about Jesus and he or she refuses to believe, there is no failure on our part. The only failure is, in fact, when we fail to be Jesus's witnesses as we have been commanded to do.

A second personal obstacle of evangelism is the fear of rejection. We are afraid that our Muslim friends will reject us if we talk about Jesus and the cross. We may twist our messages and compromise. We try to be wise and talk about Jesus only as the prophet, rather than sharing the reasons for his death and resurrection. But if we really love our Muslim friends, we will know that it is more important to share the full gospel with them, even if we risk rejection.

A third personal obstacle for evangelism is that Christians often feel inadequate. God has promised that he will give us the words to speak when the time comes. The disciples of Jesus were illiterate and not trained in theology. They were not even educated in normal schools! Yet when they spoke, the people were filled with awe because they spoke so well and so boldly. The reason why the disciples could speak so well was because they had been with Jesus and had been filled by the Holy Spirit. We need the presence of Jesus so that we can speak boldly. God is the one who will teach us to speak.

The fourth personal obstacle is a lack of passion for the lost. A popular saying is, "Nobody cares how much you know until they know how much you care." If we don't have passion and love for the lost, our unsaved Muslim friends will know it and will not be touched to respond to the gospel. When Jesus saw the lost, he was filled with so much passion for them that he wept. Let's ask God to give us this same passion for the lost.

In the end, often, our historical, materialistic, individualistic culture and our psychological, political, and spiritual restrictions get in the way of sharing the gospel. Sometimes, it's our own personal limitations and insensitivity to Muslims and "the lost" that obstructs the good news. To overcome these obstacles, Christians need to focus on Christ. Christians need to go to the Bible for encouragement, wisdom, and direction. Jesus told his disciples, "A servant is not greater than his master. If they persecuted me, they will persecute you also. If they obeyed my teaching, they will obey yours also. They will treat you this way because of my name, for they do not know the one who sent me" (John 15: 20–21, NIV).

It is fitting to close this chapter with a prayer about casting off fear. To overcome fear, we need to pray for boldness. Even the apostle Paul had to do that. "Pray also for me, that whenever I speak, words may be given me so that I will fearlessly make known the mystery of the gospel, for which I am an ambassador in chains. Pray that I may declare it fearlessly, as I should" (Ephesians 6:19–20, NIV).

Chapter 2: Why Is It Difficult for Christians to Evangelize to Shi'a Muslims?

Question for Reflection

1. Question: What causes prejudice toward Muslims?
   o Answer: Pride

2. Question: Name several historical movements that were an attempt to share the message of Christ to Muslims.
   o Answer: Crusades and Zionism

3. Question: What do Muslims use to bring blessings like money to their lives?
   o Answer: Sorcery or magic

4. Question: Do Muslims acknowledge Jesus as a prophet or a Messiah?
   o Answer: Yes, but they do *not* believe he is the son of God. In fact, they believe "God has no need of a son."

5. Question: What are some cultural differences that create misunderstandings between Christians and Muslims?
   o Answer: One example is the concept of time. Muslim's aren't interested in specific or exact designations of time, which contracts from Western culture, where being late for an appointment or for church is considered rude.

6. Question: What is the Muslim belief about marriage?
   - o Answer: It is a legal, binding contract as opposed to a sacrament.

7. Question: Name a difficult adjustment Muslims make when they move to North America.
   - o Holidays or days off work are very different from their traditions.
   - o Observing their festivals and Friday worship is difficult if they are working.

8. What makes you hesitant to share your faith with Muslims?

PART TWO

This chapter three helps the reader understand not only current and historical demographics of Shi'a Muslims, but also their history, culture, identify and practices. To be effective in evangelism and to build relationships, we must understand the people we reaching out to. What we see in the news does not represent all Muslims. Much of this chapter is more narrowly focused on the Shi'a sect of Islam, but there are many facts to be gleaned that are applicable to Islam and Muslims as a whole.

Muhammad's early life, the conception of Islam, the writing of the Qu'ran and history of the imams are explored in this chapter as well as another deeper look at the differences between Sunni and Shi'a Muslims. There is also an overview of the central beliefs as well as Islamic Articles of Faith and holy books relative to both Sunni and Shia Muslims. This chapter contains helpful timelines and graphs to help the reader grasp the content.

Most helpful, perhaps, is an overview of how Islam went from a religion to a political movement that we are perhaps most familiar with today. In a day when many Muslims tout Islam to be a "religion of peace", the reader can understand the advent of this misconception, even amongst followers of the faith.

When the Jews did not embrace his teachings, Muhammad's approach became adversarial. He stopped praying toward Jerusalem in 624 and bowed instead toward the Ka'ba in Mecca because he believed it was the shrine build by Abraham and Ishmael. His people raided Meccan caravan from 623-629, dueled with the Qoreshi clans, and then the first major battle of Badr took place in 624...and the long history of Islamic imperialism began. Islamic conquests were largely accomplished by force: convert or die; the implementation of impossibly high taxes for non-converts; and marriage to the conquered people. It is important to note that history--regardless of religious persuasion--is full of ugly, violent conquests.

The fifth shared practice is pilgrimage (Hajj) to Mecca in Saudi Arabia and is expected to occur at least once in a lifetime (Quran 2:196, 197) if they are in good health and financially able. The Hajj expresses Muslim unity and obedience to Allah. The event is based on the life of Muhammad, but many of the rituals performed there re-enact the birth of Abraham and Hagar's son, Ishmael, the spiritual patriarch of Islam.

This chapter four understands Christ's Redemption. The biggest disagreement Christians and Muslims have is about the Crucifixion. Sadly, many Christians don't fully grasp the work of the Cross and are met with seemingly valid objections and arguments from Muslims who have been taught from the time they were children to dispute this critical Truth using the Quran AND the Bible.

This chapter provides the reader with responses to these objections with powerful illustrations and analogies, biblical stories that many Muslims are familiar with, language (Arabic words and their meaning) and perhaps most effective, the use of the Quran to reveal Christ.

The first argument is by proving the Bible's inspiration, truth and morality, and inerrancy. How then do we converse with Muslims about the crucifixion? A major stumbling block preventing the Muslim from believing in Christ's redemption is the belief that the Bible was corrupted. Muslims, understandably, point to the hundreds of Bible translations. It is important to direct the Muslim's attention to the fact that the Bible is inspired by God and did not change. Open your Bible when you share Christ crucified with a Muslim. Give an answer from the word of God. Don't just challenge their thinking, but give them an exact thought from the Scriptures to wrestle with.

CHAPTER 3

SHI'A MUSLIM PERSPECTIVES AND BACKGROUNDS

Many restrictions to evangelism will not be overcome without an understanding of the Shi'a Muslim history, culture, and identity. This section will answer two main questions that Christians usually ask about Shi'a Muslims: who are the Shi'a Muslims, and how do Shi'a Muslims differ from other Muslim groups and from Christians? It is helpful for Christians to learn about Shi'a beliefs, and practices in order to more effectively witness Jesus Christ.

There are 1.6 billion Muslims worldwide, about 23 percent of the world's population. It is the fastest-growing religion, primarily because of high birth rates. The average Muslim woman has 3.1 children, although the average global rate is 2.3 children per woman. The 2050 Christian population is projected at 2.9 billion (31 percent), and the Muslim population is expected to be 2.8 billion (30 percent)—a 73 percent increase, comprising 2.1 percent of the US and 10 percent of European populations. By the year 2100, Islam is expected to be the world's largest religion.

Sixty-two percent of the world's Muslims live in the Asia-Pacific area, with large numbers in Indonesia, India, Pakistan, Bangladesh, Iran, and Turkey. Worldwide, Indonesia has the most Muslims, but by 2050, India is projected to have the highest Muslim population (with Hindu still the majority religion).

Worldwide, Shi'a Muslims make up 15–20 percent of the Muslim population. Iran's population is 90–95 percent Shiite, and in the bordering or nearby countries of Azerbaijan, Bahrain, Iraq, Yemen, Syria and Lebanon, Shiites comprise half or more of the population. There are approximately 7 million Muslims of all ages living in the United States. And by 2050, the U.S. Muslim population is projected to reach 9.1 million, with 65 percent identifying as Sunni and 11 percent as Shi'a, with 65 percent identifying as Sunni and 11 percent as Shi'a. The remaining identify as neither. The 2017 US immigration ban, however, has put a temporary halt—or at least a delay—on further immigration-based growth.

The Bible's Ishmael: Islam's Patriarch

Muslims, like many Jews and Christians, see themselves as spiritual descendants of Abraham. Here's a review of how Abraham became a father to two sons: Ishmael, who Muslims claim as the father of their faith; and Isaac, the promised seed of Abraham. God promised Abraham that he and his wife, Sarah, would have a son in their very old age. Abraham and Sarah both waivered in faith when, at Sarah's request, Abraham slept with her servant, Hagar. According to the customs of that time, any child born from that union would belong to Abraham and Sarah.

About a year later, Sarah and Abraham welcomed their own promised son, Isaac. Sarah later asked Abraham to dismiss the other mother and son from their home when Ishmael mocked Isaac. Sarah told Abraham to cast out Hagar and Ishmael. "Get rid of that slave woman and her son, for that woman's son will never share in the inheritance with my son Isaac" (Genesis 21:10, NIV). Abraham did not want to do this, but God told him, "Do not be so distressed about the boy and your slave woman. Listen to whatever Sarah tells you, because it is through Isaac that your offspring will be reckoned" (Genesis 21:12, NIV). This "nation" is Islam, according to the religion's belief. The Quran teaches that Hagar was a wife of Abraham, and she is revered as a great woman of the faith.

The Prophet's Early Life

Mohammad was born in 570 AD, in Mecca, Arabia (now Saudi Arabia). His father died before he was born; his mother died when he was six, and he lived with his grandfather until he was eight and then later lived with his uncle. Probably because of his experience as an orphan, Mohammed was sympathetic to their plight. Mohammed had no formal education, which was common at that time. He was a camel driver between Syria and Arabia then was a merchant. The Arabia peninsula today consists of the countries Yemen, Oman, Qatar, Bahrain, Kuwait, Saudi Arabia and the United Arab Emirates. During this time, he mingled with people from different nations and faiths and was heavily influenced by Judaism and Christianity.

What was his faith tradition before he grew up that would help him found what would eventually become the world's second-largest religion? There isn't a historically verifiable answer to that, but Muslim tradition teaches that Mohammed's grandfather was Abd al-Muttalib ibn Hashim, a pre-Islamic Arab group that practiced monotheism. Given the culture he grew up in, however, he could've come from a polytheistic belief system.

Career, Marriage, and Children

Muhammad was twenty-five when Khadijah, a wealthy forty-year-old widow who employed him, proposed to him. They appeared to have a very happy, monogamous marriage of twenty-five years. They had two sons, who did not survive childhood, and three daughters, though the three daughters may have been from Khadijah's previous marriages. Khadijah died in 620 AD. According to tradition, Muhammad extolled Khadijah as his favorite, and one of his later wives, Aisha, was jealous of her memory.

After Khadijah's death, Muhammad married twelve women. The Quran (4:3) allows for up to four wives, but a revelation Muhammad received allowed him to have more, and an interpretation of the Quran (33:50) is that Muhammad was allowed more than four. With the exception of Aisha, who was nine years old when they married, most of Muhammad's wives were over forty years of age, and some were widows of his companions who were slain in war. At that time in history, taking multiple wives was viewed as a charitable act to help abandoned women.

Does the Quran's allowance for polygyny (polyandry, women marrying more than one husband, is not allowed) mean most Muslims have multiple wives? It's unlikely. Although worldwide data is difficult to find, polygyny rates are affected by laws of the country and by the financial ability of the man to support more than one wife.

Many American scholars addresses criticisms of polygyny in Islam in

America: "Muslims sometimes counter western ridicule of polygyny with the accusation that more Americans have multiple wives that Muslims. The difference, they say, is that Americans take their wives in serial order, through divorce and remarriage, rather than all together." Perhaps because many of his wives were older widows, it is only recorded that Muhammad had seven children, and all his sons died in childhood.

The Birth of Islam

Cave Revelation:

Muhammad would retreat to a cave in Mount Hira (present-day Saudi Arabia), and at age forty, he had his first revelation. An angelic being forcefully told him to recite the following: "Proclaim! (or read!) in the name of thy Lord and Cherisher, who created man, out of a clot of congealed blood: Proclaim! And thy Lord is Most Bountiful—who taught by the pen—taught man that which he knew not" (Quran 96: 1–5).

Muhammad thought this experience was demonic and became suicidal, and he later sought comfort in his wife Khadijah, but she and her cousin, Nastorian priest Waraqa Ibn Nawfal (one of the four men who left the pagan faith of Mecca and returned as a Christian. Even he was claimed to be the source of the Qur'ân) convinced him that Allah, through Gabriel, was the source of the revelation. Ramadan, which means the ninth month of the Islamic calendar, was picked as the fasting month because it was during this time that Muhammad had his revelation.

A Peaceful Message, Opposed

Muhammad proclaimed a peaceful message of monotheism in Mecca for twelve years, but the majority rejected it, and the persecution for him and his followers often was violent and torturous. The introduction of Islam was a huge socioeconomic threat to the Quraysh (the dominant tribe and powerful merchant tribe of the Arabian Peninsula in the seventh century), as they benefitted from the polytheism. Mecca was a major pilgrimage center and sanctuary in the existing polytheism of Arabia, and the proclamation of monotheism threatened this whole system. Muhammad also advocated for orphans and widows and criticized the practice of burying female infants alive.

From Religion to Political Movement

A major turning point, when Islam really became a sociopolitical community, came in the year 622. Muhammad accepted an invitation from a small group of people in Medina, which was a Jewish Arab hub, two hundred miles north of Mecca. Muhammad became a community leader who helped settle disputes between feuding tribes. There, he attempted to come alongside the Jews and win them over to Islam. During his first year, his overall positive and peaceful approach continued. In fact, Judaism teachings, such as washing before praying, fasting, and divorce were "borrowed" from the Bible and can be seen in the Quran. Major portions of the Quran summarize biblical scripture, though often inaccurately. In his early evangelizing years, he had positive relationships with Jews and Christians and hoped they would recognize him as a great prophet. When asked what sign he could show to convince the Jews and Christians, he replied that his miracle was the Quran. Muhammad considered the Jewish and Christian scriptures to be true, but he claimed that they'd been misinterpreted and had corrupted their religions.

Early Quaranic verses revealed Allah's favorable view of the Jews. For example, Quran 2:62 states, "Verily! Those who believe and those who are Jews and Christians, and Sabians, whoever believes in Allah and the Last Day and does righteous good deeds shall have their reward with their Lord, on them shall be no fear, nor shall they grieve."

When the Jews did not embrace his teachings, Muhammad's approach became adversarial. He stopped praying toward Jerusalem in 624 and bowed instead toward the Ka'ba in Mecca because he believed it was the shrine build by Abraham and Ishmael. His people raided Meccan caravans from 623–629, dueled with the Qureshi clans, and then the first major battle of Badr took place in 624—and the long history of Islamic imperialism began. Islamic conquests were largely accomplished by force: either convert or die; the implementation of impossibly high taxes for nonconverts; and marriages to the conquered people. It is important to note that history, regardless of religious persuasion, is full of ugly, violent conquests.

The Sunni-Shi'a Divide

Muhammed died from illness in the year 632, at around age sixty-two. None of his sons survived to childhood, so there was no clear successor. A dispute erupted between two groups, and to this day, the main distinguishing difference between Sunni and Shi'a Islam is not about the core Islamic practices, but rather, a matter of rightful succession. It is more of a political difference than a religious one.

One group (the future Sunnites) believed that Abu Bakr, Muhammad's friend and father-in-law, should assume leadership. Some believed that he had the best political know-how to take over. The second group (the future Shi'ites), however, believed that Ali ibn Abi Talib, Mohammed's cousin, adopted son, and son-in-law, was the first male convert and was selected by Allah as the rightful heir. They argued that succession should remain within the family. He was poor, however, and disliked by the rich aristocrats of his tribe.

Caliph #1: Abu Bakr's supporters won; he was elected and took the title *Caliph*, which means spiritual leader, messenger of God, and Muhammad's successor. He died by assassination two years later, and the Muslim infighting continued. Even so, within this brief time, Muslim armies began their astonishing expansion, subduing the whole of Arabia and striking as far north as Palestine.

The succession battles continued as follows:

Sunni (meaning "People of the Tradition"):

#2: Omar, another father-in-law of Muhammad, succeeded Abu Bakr as the successor and caliph of Islam. He was murdered by another Muslim six years later.

#3: Uthman, a son-in-law of Muhammad and a Quran scribe, was chosen as the third caliph. He was assassinated by a Muslim.

Shi'a (meaning "Party of Ali"):

#4: Finally, the way was clear for (now Shi'a) Ali Ibn Abi Talib, and he assumed the fourth caliph role. However, he was opposed by Aisha, Muhammad's widow and a supporter of Sunni succession. Aisha was revered by Muslims and had a leadership role. Her forces battled Ali and lost, but Ali's forces were later attacked by (Sunni) Mu'awiya, a member of a prominent Meccan family, the Umayya. The war ended in negotiations, with some of Ali's supporters deserting him. One of these deserters killed Ali Ibn Abi Talib four years later.

#5: Mu'awiya became Caliph of the entire Muslim Sunni Empire, thus beginning the period of the Umayyad caliphate. The Umayyad caliphate ruled from 661–750.

A strong belief also began to form among Shi'as grieving followers that Ali had not died and that he would return to assume his rule. This belief in his return is like Christ's return for Christians; but for the Shi'a Muslims, it is that one of the Imams (such as Ali or Hussain—it is unknown) will return. It continued and metamorphosed into the notion of *Mahdi*, the belief that the final Imam will return at the end along with Jesus (also Hussein … that which is similar to the Christian belief in the second or the Lord of the Age). Mu'awiya became Caliph of the entire Muslim Sunnis empire, thus beginning the period of the Umayyad caliphate. Ali's Caliphate eventually provoked the first major sectarian split in the history of Islam, between two big branches Sunni and Shi'a.

During the following centuries, the two sides of Islam developed different views on politics and theology. Shi'a Muslims gave Ali a higher position than the prophet Muhammad and claimed that Islam wouldn't spread, and that the unbelieving wouldn't be defeated without Ali. However, they claimed that he and his children, and especially Hussein, were redeemers to defend Islam after the death of the prophet Muhammad. The prophet Muhammad used to call Hussein and his brother Hassan his beloved sons.

Imams: Central to Shi'a Theology

It is easy to confuse the meanings of Caliph and Imam. Here are some definitions:

Sunni and Shi'a Caliph: The successor of Muhammad, but they disagree on who that was. The Sunnis and Shi'a only share recognition of Ali and Hussein.

Sunni Imams: Religious and community leaders who provide wisdom and guidance.

Shi'a Imams: The early caliphs are recognized as Shi'a Imams, with a saintlike, revered status. The Shi'a Muslims believe that the Imam is someone who can lead mankind in all aspects of life. They believe their Imams are ordained, anointed, and chosen by God and not by men. Their status is like Catholicism's pope. Sunnis, on the other hand, view Imams as devout Muslims with strong faith in the holy books, but they are not elevated to the same godlike status. Instead, they are regarded as community and mosque leaders.

Each of these Imams is considered perfect in doctrine and practice, and they provide divine leadership to the community of the faithful. They believe that the prophet Muhammad and the Imams who succeeded him must also uphold the highest standard of justice. They also believe that an Imam is a perfect example in everything and that he must be followed since he is appointed by Allah.

The following are some views of Imams:
1. They are like God.
2. The Imam knows his hour of death.
3. No one possesses complete knowledge of Holy Quran except Imams.
4. The Imam was assumed to have special secret knowledge necessary to understand the secret meanings of the scripture.
5. The present Quran is abridged whereas the original Quran is kept by the Imam Mehdi.
6. The future Imam prophesied who would rule for before Judgement Day.
7. All Imams are equal in rank and status to Prophet Muhammad.

The hierarchy of the twelve Shi'a Imams is family-driven. After

Ali's death, his eldest son, Hassan, accepted an allowance in return for not pursuing his claim to the Caliph. He died within a year, allegedly poisoned. Ali's younger son, Hussein, agreed to put his claim to the Caliph on hold until Mu'awiya's death. He was defeated and killed at Karbala, in modern-day Iraq. His death cemented the deep, lasting division among Muslims that persist to this day. However, when Mu'awiya finally died in the year 680, his son Yazid took over the Caliph. Yazid sent a message to Medina to ask the people to recognize him as the leader. He instructed his army that if anyone refused to give allegiance to him, they would be killed. He also name Hussein as one of the most important people to talk to first. After summoning him, he asked Hussein to submit his will to Yazid. Hussein refused and decided to leave with his family (his wife, children, brothers, and some others) to Iraq because he knew that Yazid already planned to assassinate him. Yazid arranged a huge army of thirty-three thousand men, who were very well equipped, to surround Hussein and his family. Hussein had just over a hundred men with him, and most of them were among his family. They forced Hussein and his family to retreat to Karbala. Karbala is a two-phrased word: kar means sorrow, and bala means vexation. Hussein, his family, and men were slaughtered at the Battle of Karbala (in modern-day Iraq). Hussein was beheaded, and his head was taken to the Sunni Caliph in Damascus.

The Shi'a view Hussein as a major hero and the greatest of martyrs. His death represented a significant turning point and line in the Sunni-Shi'a division. Some of Hussein's followers claimed that he had not died and that he would return, and his death is recognized every year in Ashura as a ritualistic event. Meanwhile, the Shi'a acknowledged Hussein's son Zayn al-Abidin as their Imam.

The House of Ali and the Shi'a Twelve Imams

Hashim

Abd al-Muttalib

Al-'Abbas-----------------Abu Talib-----------------'Abd Allah

Ali-------------(Cousin)----------**Muhammad**

(1) Ali (600–661)------(wife) Fatima

(2) Hasan (625–669)

(3) Hussein (626–680)

55

(4) Ali Zain al-Abideen (658–713)
(5) Muhammad al-Baqir (676–743)
(6) Jafar al-Saddiq (703–765)
(7) Musa al-Qazim (745–799)
(8) Ali al-Radi (765–818)
(9) Muhammad al-Taqi (810–835)
(10) Ali al-Hadi (827–868)
(11) Hasan al-Askari (846–874)
(12) Muhammad al-Muntazar (868–present)

Shi'a sect

The Shi'a have numerous sects, with 85 percent of Shia's belonging to the Twelvers. The second-largest group is the Seveners. The tie that binds all sects is that they believe that the only true rulers of the Islamic community can be direct descendants of the prophet. Each sect, however, has a set of beliefs that may differ from another; but the biggest differentiation is the number of Imams they recognize to be legitimate, who they recognize those Imams to be, and what roles those Imams possess.

Most Shia sects recognize the first four Imams:

1. Ali ibn Abu Talib,
2. Hassan ibn Ali,
3. Husayn ibn Ali, and
4. Zayn al-Abidin.

In accordance with their names, the Twelvers recognize twelve Imams; the Seveners recognize seven, and the Fivers recognize five. The Twelvers believe that the twelfth and final Imam, Muhammad al-Mahdi, underwent a period of occultation and will remain hidden from the world until the Day of Judgement, when he will return to help redeem the world from sin.

Shi'a Beliefs and Practices

The Shi'a Muslims doctrines divide into two main categories. The first category is *Roots of the Religion*, and the second category is *Branches of the Religion*, or *the practices*.

Roots of the Religion

The central doctrine of Islam is the oneness of God—that there is only one God, and that no partner is to be associated with him. The Quran states, "He is Allah," The One and Only; Allah, the Eternal, Absolute; He begot not, nor is He begotten" (Quran 112:1–4). The "Allah" of Islam is content with himself and has no direct relationship with man. To Shi'as specifically, Allah is transcendent, and when the Shi'a feel that Allah is near, it scares them to death. He is frightening to all Muslims; his role is more of judgement than of love. Shi'a Muslims are taught that Allah can inflict punishment on them at any time. For those reasons and more, Shi'a Muslims look to their Imams and leaders for their wisdom on what is forbidden and what earns you credit with Allah. Like with Catholics, who ask for Mary's intercession, Shi'a Muslims pray to Imams.

Another principle is divine justice. The Shi'a school of Islamic thought values justice so highly that the belief in justice has becomes its seal in theological books. It's believed that Allah is just in his dealings with mankind, that Allah does not oblige anyone to believe or to disbelieve in Him, and that Allah does not compel human beings to do good or evil. It is entirely left upon people to make the right choice by considering the guidance provided by the prophets and Imams. Based on this emphasis of the concept of justice, Shi'a Muslims are not permitted to cooperate or work with unjust rulers, and they are also expected to strive for a just social order in human society. This is the underlying basis of the various Shi'a movements in history in which they have risen against the rulers and governments of their own times.

Leadership. Traditionally, Najaf, Iraq, has held the leadership headquarters for the Shi'a Muslims. The seat of the "Shi'a Marja" is the second-highest authority on religion and law for the Shi'a after the prophet Muhammad and the Imams. The main leader is the Grand Ayatollah, Ali Al-Sistani, who sits in Najaf and is widely revered by Shi'ites throughout the world. Most Shi'ites follows the Najaf leadership. There are more Shi'ites in South Asia than there are in Iran, and almost all are followers of the Najaf leadership, indicating that Najaf is more important than Qom (the seat of Iran's Islamic leadership) to Shi'a Islam.

Also, Al-Ahwaz (Khuzestan province in south western Iran) has the third-largest Arab Shi'a population after Iraq and Yemen, with 3.9 million.

Al-Ahwazi Grand Ayatollahs also have traditionally followed the Najaf leadership, emphasizing the region's cultural autonomy from Iran's centers of power. Soon after Iran's Islamic Revolution, the Ahwazi Grand Ayatollah Muhammad Taher al-Khaqani led a rebellion against the country's new rulers, calling for Ahwazi autonomy and minority rights. The rebellion was put down, and he was held under house arrest in Qom on Ayatollah Khomeini's orders. He died in 1986 while still under house arrest. He left a brother, Sheikh Eisa al-Khaqani, who fled to Iraq and later to the UAE, where he currently resides and continues his brother's political work against the Iranian regime and its religious leadership. He has two sons, and he has moved in a political direction, believing that Arab Shi'ites should speak out against the Iranian regime.

In order to become a religious leader (*mujtahid* مجتهد), it is necessary to complete a rigorous and lengthy course of religious studies in one of the important schools in Iran or Iraq and to receive an authorization from a qualified *mujtahid*. These canonical schools are called *Fiqh's* فقه. The only *Fiqh's* in Shi'a Islam are Usuli, Akhbari, and Shaykhi. These three all belong to the majority Twelvers sect. A student goes through the ranks from preacher to mujtahid, until he becomes a *source* or *ayatollah*, and thereafter, the *greater ayatollah*. A comparison can be made between the traditional American academic track: from bachelor's to master's to PhD degrees.

Islamic leaders in the West can also change the laws and traditions to suit Shi'a Muslims' needs. For example, Muslims in the United States disapprove of what happened on September 11, 2001. They say that violence is not acceptable in true Islam. But, at the same time, some of them sympathize with Muslim extremists who allow little children to be exposed to teachings of the extremist leaders in the Middle East like "the sword in one hand and Quran in the other" and who support violence. They are tolerant of men killing themselves and innocent people just for the promise of rewards in heaven.

Another central belief concerns the prophets. *Al-anbiya'* الأنبياء. In Arabic, there is a distinction between *prophet* and *messenger*. According to Islamic tradition, a total of 124,000 prophets have been sent to warn and guide mankind. All these prophets essentially preached the same faith. The Quran mentions twenty-five of them. Most are unknown, but some include biblical personages, such as Adam, David, Solomon, Jonah, John the Baptist, and Jesus. However, Muhammad is the only one who is viewed as both a prophet and messenger.

One final core belief is the last Day of Judgment. Shi'a believe that Allah will resurrect all of mankind to be judged. Judgment is the main theme in the Quran, and it is emphasized in about 14 percent of the verses. Good deeds will be weighed in the balance against bad deeds. All people will be judged according to their deeds (Quran 2:62). But Shi'a Muslims believe they have special favor with Allah because their lineage is from the family of Muhammad. they anticipate a special bargain.

Common Beliefs and Practices of Shi'a and Sunni

The first common practice is the statement of faith. They both proclaim that "there is no god but Allah and Muhammad is the messenger of Allah." Shi'as, however, add on a couple of sentences: "Ali the friend and companion of Allah, Caliph of Muhammad without detachment or severance."

The second common practice is prayer. Shi'a Muslims follow the same prayer ritual as Sunnis. The five prayers are in the dawn, midday, midafternoon, sunset, and nightfall. The Shi'a pray five times but in a different format (1 + 2 +2) = 5. They pray at dawn and then combine midday and midafternoon together, and they also combine the sunset and nightfall prayers together.

The third common practice is alms-giving. Giving to the poor in Islam means giving back to Allah. All Muslims are expected to give 2.5 percent of their yearly savings. The alms are given to the poor and those in need or distress, and it may also be spent for the cause of Allah (Quran 9:60). Many Muslims believe alms-giving brings special rewards in heaven and cleanses a person from his mistakes or from wrongdoing. According to Shi'a practice, one-fifth is the acceptable amount.

The fourth common practice is fasting. Fasting for Muslims is practiced in the form of a month-long period in Ramadan, which, by definition, is the ninth month of the year. Ramadan celebrates the first revelation of the Quran to Muhammad by the Angel Gabriel. It was set down in the Quran as a guide to mankind. Every Muslim is expected to spend that month fasting from food, drink, smoking, and sex, from sunrise to sunset.

The fifth shared practice is pilgrimage (*Hajj*) to Mecca in Saudi Arabia, which is expected to occur at least once in a lifetime (Quran 2:196–197) if they are in good health and financially able. The *Hajj* expresses Muslim unity and obedience to Allah. The event is based on the life of Muhammad, but many of the rituals performed there reenact the birth of Abraham and Hagar's son, Ishmael, the spiritual patriarch of Islam.

In addition to the pilgrimage to Mecca, Shi'a Muslims make pilgrimages to Iraq to the tombs of the Imams—especially Hussein's. The holy day of Ashoura is commemorated by the Shi'a as a day of mourning for the martyrdom of Hussein. Shi'ite Muslim men, women, and even children march along streets, some beating their chests and slashing their heads with blades. This self-flagellation, however, is forbidden by Sunni Muslims. The marches in Lebanon, Bahrain, Saudi Arabia, Iraq, and Iran have taken place in an atmosphere of tension between Shi'a Muslims and Sunni Muslims that has risen again during the past years as they struggle for power in the Middle East.

Another common practice is jihad. Within Islam, there are differing interpretations of what jihad means. The word *jihad* is often translated as *holy war*, but it literally means *struggle, striving,* or *exertion*. The jihad, in its religious context, always involves a fight against evil. Most Muslims accept the concept of struggle; this may manifest in an internal spiritual, psychological, social, physical, and even intellectual struggle (Quran 2:190–194; 4:74, 76; 8:12, 39–42; 8:15,16; 9:39; 9:5). Not all accept that it means a war against the enemies of Islam. Jihad in Islam may take many forms: jihad of the heart involves fighting our sinful tendencies so that we can obey the law, the five pillars, the Hadith, and the Quran.

Physical jihad is violence and proclaims war against Christians, Jews, or any nation that does not agree with Muslim teaching. The Quran teaches that Muslims have the right to attack nonbelievers (Quran 2:191–193; 4:76; 4:89; 4:95; 4:104; 5:33; 8:12; 8:15; 8:39; 8:57; 8:59–60; 9:5; 9:14; 9:20; 9:29–30; 9:38–39; 9:41–42; 9:73; 9:88; 9:11; 9:123; 17:16; 18:65–81; 25:52; 33:60–62; 47:3–4; 47:35; 48:17; 48:29; 61:4; 61:10–12; 66:9) in any season, in any land, and at any time. *Jihad of the mouth* is making proclamations in the mosques, in the media, in debates, and in verbal arguments. It also involves curses against the enemy. Usually, we see this in Islamic countries when Shi'a protest and say words like "death to Israel" or other offending countries. *Jihad of the pen* applies to literature and theological books written against the faith of Christians, Jews, or against any other religion, in defense of the Islamic faith and the Quran. Finally, there is the *Jihad of fatwa*, or *lies and deception*.

Additional Practices of Shi'a Muslims

Shi'a Muslims add additional practices that they call *religion branches*. The first additional practice is to enjoy what is good and to forbid what is wrong. It is used often in the Quran. This expression is the basis of the Islamic institution of hisbah, and sometimes it is referred to by this word. Hisbah forms a central part of Islamic Shi'a doctrine. Men of hisbah are people who devote their time to denouncing visible evil either voluntarily or by paying into the treasury of the Muslims. Part of their job is to denounce evil actions in the marketplaces and elsewhere. They are expected to force others not to sin and to force them to do "well."

Another practice is forbidding what is evil. Those who do not prevent evil by their hearts, tongues, and hands is like a dead person among the living. They are two creatures—for those who help and follow them, Allah honors them; and for those who neglect them, Allah disgraces them. In practice, the Shi'a are divided by some who believe that one should not take social postures unless the Imam or one of the Shi'a religious leaders specifically orders it.

Another added practice is disassociating. The Shi'a Muslims' disassociation doctrine is referring to the obligation of hating those who hate Allah and cursing those who reject the community of Shi'a. According to Shi'a, it is obligatory to disassociate oneself from a person who has committed atrocities against the prophet Muhammad and his family. This additional aspect is manipulated to protect their faith, and within the Shi'ite Islamic tradition, the concept of *Taqiyyah* refers to a dispensation, allowing believers to conceal their faith when under threat, persecution, or pressure.

The final additional practice pertains to immigration. A Shi'a who is born and raised in a Muslim country, where he consciously and subconsciously absorbs the laws, values, and teachings of Islam, grows up into a young person who is aware of the customs of his religion, follows its path, and is led by its guidance. On the other hand, a Muslim who is born and brought up in a non-Muslim country demonstrates the influence of that environment very clearly in his thoughts, ideas, behavior, values, and etiquette unless Allah helps him. This un-Islamic influence is seen more in the second generation of those who have migrated to non-Muslim countries. It is because of these influences that the Shi'a's view of immigration is reflected in many Shi'a's books (*hadith*). It literally means "becoming shorn of one's percepts of faith after migrating," or leaves the faith of Shi'a. Such a migration is counted as one of the major sins. The Shi'a Muslims religious leaders, jurists, make rules for the migration to non-Muslim countries.

> It is forbidden or sin (haram) to travel to non-Muslim countries in the East or the West if that journey causes loss of the faith of an Arab Shi'a Muslim, no matter whether the purpose of that journey is tourism, business, education, or residence of a temporary or permanent nature. It is recommended for an Arab Shi'a Muslim to travel to non-Muslim countries for the purpose of spreading the religion of Islam and its teaching, provided that he can safe guard himself and his young children against the dangers of loss of the faith. If an immigrant fears the loss of faith for his children, is it forbidden (haram) for him to stay in that non-Muslim country? Yes, the same rule applies to himself also. Is it obliged (wajib) on the immigrants in Europe and America (and other similar countries) to strive for teaching their children Arabic, and that ignorance of Arabic may lead in the future to ignorance of the main Islamic body of knowledge, and that will naturally lead to less familiarity with religious teachings and loss of faith? To teach them Arabic is wajib only to the extent which is necessary for performing their religious duties that have to be done in Arabic. What do the jurists mean when they speak of, "loss of faith"? It means either committing a forbidden act by indulging in minor or major sins like drinking intoxicant, adultery, eating forbidden meat, or drinking najis (نجس) (impure

drink). It also means abandoning the fulfillment of a compulsory act like neglecting praying, fasting, hajj and other obligations. The journey would not have a negative impact on his faith and the faith of those who are related to him. Arab Shi'a is residing in North America does not become a hurdle in the of fulfilling his religious obligations toward himself and his family presently as well as in future. If the wife, boys or girls strongly feels or is sure that her travelling with the husband to a non-Muslim country will result in loss of faith, it is forbidden (haram) for her to travel with him. A son is not allowed to disobey his parents when they forbid him from travelling, if their refusal to give permission is out of their concern for the son, or if his journey will cause distress to them because of his separation from them - provided that he does not suffer loss by not travelling. (Muhammad Taqi, 1998)

Similarities and Differences Between Sunni and Shi'a

The major differences between the two main sects of Muslims are still relevant today, and are important to understand if we are going to undertake evangelism. Sunnis and Shi'a Muslims agree on the core fundamentals of Islam, the Five Pillars of Sunni Islam, and with some exceptions, recognize each other as Muslims. But they are different branches of the faith, as is the case with Protestantism and Catholicism.

The primary difference between the Shi'a and Sunni is what constitutes proper succession, or the transfer of power after Muhammad's death. The Shi'a Muslims believe that Muhammad had announced Ali, his cousin, as his heir at least two months before his impending death. The Sunnis do not recognize this incident and have splintered from the Shi'a primarily over this question. This understanding of the Caliph and leadership after the demise of Muhammad is the foremost difference between the two sects. Many Sunni books record an incident in which the prophet returned from his last pilgrimage, or *Hajj*, at a place called Ghadir-al-Khum, publicly—in front of ten thousand people—announced Ali to be his heir.

The Quran is the word of God revealed to Muhammad and is the primary text for Muslims. It literally means *Recitation*. It is the foundation and the core of Islam, and it is believed to be perfect. Muslims believe that the Quran came by recitation to Muhammad from the angel Gabriel in Mecca in 610 AD. All Muslims believe that the Quran is composed of 114 *Suras,* or chapters. Although both groups read the Quran, Sunnis believe the Quran is complete, while most Shi'a Muslims believe that the present-day Quran is incomplete and is missing the fourth part. They believe that the remaining part is hidden with the Imam Muhammad in his cave burial site.

An obvious difference can be seen in the proclamation of faith. Sunnis do it by saying, "There is no god but Allah, and Muhammad is the messenger of Allah." Shi'as add on a couple of sentences, saying, "Ali is the friend and companion of Allah, Caliph of Muhammad without detachment or severance."

The Shi'a Muslims also have some different *Hadith,* or sayings of Muhammad, and prefer those narrated by Ali and Fatima to those related by other companions of the prophet. The *Sunnah* (meaning *sayings and deeds*) of the prophet of Islam is, after the Quran, the main source of guidance for the Sunni Muslims.

The word *Shi'ite* means *partisan* and indicates that Shi'ites are partisans of Ali. An important distinction between the two branches is that although the Shi'a glorify Muhammad, they believe some of the glory belongs to Ali and the twelve Imams. They take the glory that Sunnis give to Muhammad and transfer some of it to Ali, his sons, the twelve Imams, and, to some extent, to their spiritual leaders.

Shi'ites also differ from the Sunnis regarding the authority of the Imams. In many ways, Ali and his sons are more important than the other Caliphs. Unlike the Sunnis, Shi'ite Muslims believe that the Islamic leader, whom they call the Imam, is more than merely a guardian of Muhammad's prophetic legacy; Imam's spiritual abilities enable him to interpret the Quran and to lead the Islamic community infallibly, and they are the true guardians of the people. The Shi'a Imam has come to be filled with pope-like infallibility, and the Shi'a religious hierarchy is not dissimilar in structure and religious power to that of the Catholic Church within Christianity. Sunni Islam, in contrast, more closely resembles the independent churches of American Protestantism. Sunnis do not have a formal clergy, just scholars and jurists who may offer nonbinding opinions.

Shi'a Muslims believe that their supreme Imam is a fully spiritual guide, inheriting some of Muhammad's inspiration. He is called Muhammad al-Mahdi. Shi'as refuse to accept that the al-Mahdi has died, preferring to believe that he was merely "hidden" and will return. Shi'a theology is distinguished by its glorification of Ali. The best-known modern example of the Shi'a supreme Imam is the late Ayatollah Khomeini, whose portrait hangs in many Shi'a Muslims' homes.

Further, Shi'a Islam permits temporary marriage, which is forbidden by the Sunnis of today. Temporary marriage was originally permitted at the time of the prophet and is promoted by some Shi'a. Temporary marriage allows a man to marry a woman with the intention of divorcing her after a time, even just a couple of days. According to the Sunnis, this is totally unacceptable.

The Ka'ba, in Mecca, is the symbolic House of God. All Muslims must face its direction whenever they stand for their daily prayers. Visiting Mecca is necessary for the forgiveness of sins. Shi'a Muslims also believe that visiting the shrines of the Imams and other pious saints is an act of great importance, but not for the Sunnis. Shi'as are much more interested in eschatological events and have some unique ideas about what will happen at the end of the world—much like the various dispensational ideas of the end of the world among certain evangelicals.

The following chart compares the similarities and differences between the major Islamic branches, Shi'a and Sunni. This chart of information is generalized and should not be used as the only basis of information:

Theme	Sunni	Shi'a
Approximate population	1.5 billion (80–90 percent)	300 million (15–20 percent)
Geography	The majority in most Muslim countries	Half or more of population in Iran, Azerbaijan, Pakistan, Bahrain, Iraq, and Lebanon
Meaning of name	"Path" or "tradition"	"Party" or "Followers" of Ali, or the house of Ali
Sacred Books	Quran (means "Recitation"); Hadith ("narrative") and Sunnah	Primarily the Quran, the Hadith, and the Shia Jurisprudence (fiqh)

The Split and Correct Origins	Abu Bakr, companion and father-in-law of Muhammad, elected by people of Medina as first caliph	Family lineage: Ali Muhammad's cousin, son-in-law, and fourth caliph, and twelve imams
Theology	Four major schools of Muslim law are recognized	The twelve Imams were perfect interpreters of the Quran
Articles of Belief	One God; angels, prophets, and holy books (Quran and Hadith); the Day of Judgement; God's predestination	One God (Oneness) (Tawhid): Justice, prophethood, Imamah (leadership); and the Day of Resurrection
Pillars of Faith	Statement of faith, prayer, fasting on Ramadan, pilgrimage to Mecca, and Zakah (alms tax)	Statement of faith, prayer, fasting during Ramadan, pilgrimage to Mecca, and the holiest sites of Najaf and Karbala are the most revered by Shias and charity
Prayer Practices	Five prayers, five times daily	Five prayers, three times daily
Special day of prayer	Friday	Friday
Eschatology	The ideas of life after death, matters of the soul, and the Day of Judgement, known as *Yawm al-Qiyāmah*	The messiah known as the "Twelfth Imam" or the "Mahdi" will appear soon to establish a global Islamic kingdom known as the caliphate
Marriage	Men can marry up to four wives; temporary marriage is forbidden	Men can marry up to four wives; temporary marriage is allowed
Terrorism	Islamic Brethren in Egypt and Turkey; Al-Qaeda in Yemen and Libya; Hamas in Palestine, ISIS/ISIL in Syria, Iraq, and North Africa; Taliban in Afghanistan; and Boko-Haram in Nigeria and South Africa	Hezbollah in Lebanon, Iraq; Houthi, in Yemen; and Revolutionary Guard Corps/Quds Force in Iran
Leaders and Authority	Human leaders elected from the Ummah (Muslim community by consensus). Imam is a prayer leader; no clerical hierarchy	Prophet is appointed by God alone—only God has the prerogative to appoint the successor to his prophet. Twelve Imams are infallible and have God's authority

End Times. The Future Imam Al-Mahdi	The concept of a Mahdi is not an essential doctrine in Sunni Islam	He already came, and he is hidden Imam. He will appear at the end of time to rule over the world

Major Similarities and Differences Between Shi'a Muslim and Christians

What's the common ground between Muslims and Christians? First and foremost, the Christian response should be that we're all sinners who need a savior: "For all have sinned and fall short of the glory of God" (Romans 3:23, NIV). We all are humans, affected by our culture and upbringing, who ultimately long for a sense of peace and belonging. Regardless of disagreements on immigration, Christians are called to "love your neighbor as yourself" (based on Mark 12:31, NIV).

The relationship between Islam and Christianity is a relevant concern. It is a concern in our world, given the ongoing problems in the Muslim world; Iraq, Lebanon, Palestine, Afghanistan, and Pakistan and the major roles that the government of the United States is playing against in the Muslim world. It is a concern for Christians in North America and for many of us on a personal level, the Shi'a Muslim people are people we work with, live near, and who our children perhaps go to school with. Nevertheless, Shi'a Muslims and Christians have extremely different, but sometimes similar views on major points of ideology and theology. These differences between them are never an excuse for political, social, and cultural hatred. For Christians, none of these differences can stand as barriers of loving, befriending, and sharing the full gospel with Muslims.

Similarities
The following are main similarities between Christianity and Islam:

- Moral living, sacrifices, and doing good to others.
- There is one God. And that God is sovereign; He rules history.
- The existence of angels.
- Many of the same prophets, such as Adam, Noah, Abraham, and David.
- Heaven, hell, and judgement.

Differences

The main difference between Muslims and Christians is the perceptions of Almighty God and Christ.

The Word of God. Both Muslims and Christians agree that it is impossible for God to change and cannot inspire error in his word. Yet, Muslims replace the Torah, Zabur (Psalms), and Injil (the gospel) with the Quran. They contend that only the Quran has been preserved in an uncorrupted state. They believe that the Old and New Testaments are no longer reliable as God's word to man because of corruption. They also point out that the Bible has hundreds of translations. Like with Roman Catholics and Orthodox, they do not adhere to Sola Scripture—or scripture alone. The Quran is the most sacred, but the Hadith (or sayings of Muhammad) and Sunnah (the way Muhammad lived) are followed. Despite having what they consider to be God's word, their traditions and interpretations take precedence over the written text.

The Quran claims that the Torah of Moses and the Psalms of David were corrupted and that God had to send the gospels because the Jews were a stiff-necked, disobedient people. He scattered them all over the world and sent Jesus to establish a new book and Christianity. Later, however, in the seventh century, the Quran teaches that Christianity had become so corrupt that God sent the promised one whom Jesus talked about in John 14. Christians know this promised one is the Holy Spirit, but Islam teaches that his name is Muhammad, and he established Islam, God's final revelation.

One God, in Three. Both religions worship one God, but Muslims do not define Christians as true monotheists. Christians recognize the trinity as God in three persons: Father, Son, and Holy Spirit. Even so, the unity of the trinity is hard for many Christians to fully grasp, so it is no surprise that Muslims don't believe it. The trinity reminds Muslims of paganism since many believe that Christians worship three Gods (Allah, Jesus, and Mary). Regardless of the true meaning and that Mary is not part of the trinity, the Muslim response is that the "three" comes down to multiple gods. They call it *Al-shirk*, or polytheism, and according to the Quran, it is the one unforgivable sin. Anyone who commits this sin will be condemned to death and to hell in the afterlife.

The Name of God. The Arabic definition of *Allah* is *God* or *the God* and was a deity used long before Muhammad claimed it as the name of Islam's God. Historical records show that Christians used *Allah* to refer to their God, and today, Arabic Christians use *Allah* to describe the triune God they worship. It is recognized, however, that the two Gods are indeed very different and that clarification is needed in cultures where *Allah* is used by both Muslims and Christians. Arabic Christians, for example, may use Allah is One in combination with *al-Ab,* meaning *God the Father, Al-Ibn, meaning God the Son and Al-Ruh Al-Qudus, meaning God the Holy Spirit* And, of course, there are other names that can be used to describe the Christian God, such as *Yahweh* or *Jehovah*, which literally means, "He who will be."

Relationship. The relationship between Allah and man is not relational and is not based on love. Muslims see Allah as unaffected by sin. On one hand, Allah knows the future home of all people, heaven or hell, but Muslims still must work hard to earn Allah's favor and to be cleansed of their sins. No Muslim knows his or her destiny but works hard to earn Allah's favor. According to Quran 46:9, Muhammad himself didn't know his destiny. This is in contrast with the view of the Christian God, who sent his son to die for the sins of the world—a faith based on the grace of God. Because of the God who sent his son to take our place, we can rest in the knowledge that our citizenship in heaven is based on his work on the cross.

Free Will. Allah decreed everything before creation and now watches it unfold. Man has no freedom of choice. Yahweh, however, gave Adam the freedom of choice and teaches mankind to choose well. For example, God allows Adam to name the animals (Genesis 2:19–20), and he chose to disobey God.

Muslims believe that on the seventh day, God was on his throne and did not need to rest, as Christians claim. God created the earth as it is now, with good and evil, death and suffering. He created Adam to be weak and in need of guidance. As a result, Muslims are justified to cease work for Friday prayers. Christians believe that God made the seventh day holy and a day of rest and remembrance of God (Genesis 2:2–3; Acts 20:7). God created the earth entirely good, without evil (Genesis 1:31; 1 Timothy 4:4). Death and suffering entered the world because of Satan's deception of Eve and Adam, which introduced sin to the world (Genesis 3:14–19; Romans 5:12, 6:23; James 1:13–15).

Sin. Islam does not teach about the original sin. There are classes of sin: slips, lapses, offenses, and transgressions. Ultimately, Allah is the cause of sin (Quran 4:88; 14:4; 16:93; 35:8). Christians believe that sin entered the world through Adam (Romans 5:12, NIV: "Sin entered the world through one man ..."), but the Quran teaches that Adam repented of his sin, and that, in essence, his sin ended there and was not passed down to his ancestors. Muslims believe that they make their own choices to follow Allah and to avoid sin. Because of this belief, atonement for sin is not needed.

The Quran teaches that Allah created Adam in Paradise and made him his *viceroy* (Caliph) over the earth. Adam sinned and repented, and God forgave him. People are forgetful of Allah's law and, ultimately, every good and evil action is the result of predestination. Fellowship with Allah is impossible, and his relationship with humans is determined by his election and their obedience to his laws. Allah rewards and loves those who please Him.

Jesus, "Son of God." Muslims call Jesus *Isa, the son of Mary*, and believe he was a great prophet, that he was born of a virgin, raised the dead, performed miracles, was holy and faultless, and the Shiites believe that he may be the Imam who returns to judge at the end of time. They reject the idea that he is the son of God. To say that God has a son is blasphemous: "Warn those who say, 'God has taken to Himself a son ... a monstrous word it is, issuing out of their mouths; they say nothing but a lie" (Quran 18:4–5).

The Cross. Shi'a Muslims deny the cross and the resurrection because they misunderstand the loving nature of God. Shi'a Muslims believe that Christ was not crucified, and that the Jews crucified a substitute. A Christian who talks to a Shi'a Muslim about Christ's crucifixion and redemption may find that the Muslim smiles silently. They believe the son of Mary did not die on a cross, and they think it was Judas Iscariot who was crucified (Quran 4:157). Some Shi'a Muslim groups think a disciple of Christ volunteered to take Christ's place, and some say a Jewish bystander was mistakenly crucified instead. Other Muslims believe that a Roman soldier was made to look like Jesus and was crucified. And some Shi'a

Muslims believed Allah lifted Christ up to Himself (Quran 3:55, 4:158). Some of our Shi'a Muslim friends who saw *The Passion of the Christ* told us that Jesus's death was just like that of the martyr Hussein. Despite this, they still held to the Islamic teaching that Jesus was not crucified.

Salvation and Judgment. The Quran professes that salvation is obtained through works. The Quran gives Muslims what is good and bad, what are righteous deeds and sinful deeds, and the norms for daily life. Upon death, each person's deeds will be weighed in the balance. In Islam, there are two ways to get to paradise: for most, your good deeds are weighed against your bad deeds. If you have done enough good deeds when compared to your bad deeds, you will eventually get to paradise after spending some time burning in the fires of hell (Quran 19:67–68, 71–72). The second way is to die as a martyr, defending Islam.

The Bible presents a picture of a God who suffers because of his disobedient people. He is grieved, and he is angered. The Bible uses *the salvation* term in a specific way to refer to ultimate redemption from sin and reconciliation to God. In this context, then, salvation is from the ultimate calamity of God's judgment. It is Jesus Christ, the savior, who "delivers us from the wrath to come" (1 Thessalonians 1:10).

Fasting. The fast is used by Muslims to teach patience and self-control, and to please Allah and show submission to him. Most importantly, the fast is seen as a great sign of obedience by the Muslims to Allah. Hadith, the sayings and actions of Muhammad, says, "Whoever observes fasts during the month of Ramadan out of sincere faith, and hoping to attain Allah's rewards, and then all his past sins will be forgiven" (*Hadith Sahih Bukhari*).

Fasting in Christianity is not compulsory but is encouraged. Fasting is not considered a good work or deed to pay for our sin. It is not the way of salvation. Fasting may be a sign of repentance, but it is not done to earn forgiveness.

Prayer. Prayer consists of recitations from the Quran. The Quran says prayer "restrains from the shameful and unjust deed" (29:45). Without prayers, one ceases to be a true Muslim. Muslims must pray five times a day, at dawn, midday, midafternoon, sunset, and nightfall. As stated earlier, Shi'a Muslims also pray five times a day, but the prayers are condensed into three sessions. Prayer must take place wherever the Muslim is, alone or with other Muslims, but preferably in a congregation.

Prayer is one of the most valuable assets we have as Christians. God allows us to partner with him to fulfill his purposes on the earth. Prayer in Christianity is a way of communication and is much more than simply giving God a list of stuff you want him to do, although sometimes it can be like that. It is an opportunity to spend time enjoying God's company, a bit like you would do with your best friend, asking questions, talking about your family and friends, wondering about the future, saying sorry, saying thank you, listening, being comfortable with silence, and just being glad to be in his presence.

Chapter 3: Shi'a Muslim Perspectives and Backgrounds
Questions for Reflection:

1. How did the Shi'a religion start?

2. Why does Shi'a love Ali? How does Shi'a view of Aisha?

3. What did the Shi'a believe?

4. How do Shi'a view sin?

5. How do the Shi'a pray?

6. Do Sunnis believe in Imam Mahdi?

7. Is Imam Mahdi Shi'a or Sunni?

8. Who is the eleventh Imam?

9. What do Muslims think of Christians?

CHAPTER 4

UNDERSTANDING CHRIST'S REDEMPTION

"It is for freedom that Christ has set us free ..." (Galatians 5:1, NIV)

"Faith comes from hearing the message, and the message is heard through the word about Christ." (Romans 10:17, NIV)

There are several issues that Christians and Shi'a Muslims disagree about, but the biggest one is the crucifixion. Muslims declare this event to be untrue. In order to explain Christ's crucifixion to a Muslim, or, more particularly, to a Shiite, one would have to understand the Shi'a Muslim's basic line of reasoning and assumptions about God, Christ, and his plan for salvation to humanity. This section will answer the following questions:

- What do Shi'a Muslims believe regarding Jesus's death?
- Who is Christ to them?
- How do we share Jesus's redemption?

I will reveal proofs through the Bible and the Quran to prove that Christ was crucified. I will also find evidences for Christ's death on the cross in order to build a logical means of sharing that Jesus was crucified.

The hatred in Islam toward the cross of our redeemer, Jesus, has its roots deep in a collective bondage, which cannot be overcome with logic alone. The cross is always one of the greatest stumbling blocks for Muslims and will offend many. "For since in the wisdom of God the world did not know him, God was pleased through the foolishness of what was preached to save those who believe. Jews demand signs and Greeks look for wisdom, but we preach Christ crucified: a stumbling block to Jews and foolishness to Gentiles, but to those whom God has called, both Jews and Greeks, Christ the power of God and the wisdom of God. For the foolishness of God is wiser than human wisdom and the weakness of God is stronger than human strength" (1 Corinthians 1:21–25, NIV).

What Do Muslims Believe Regarding Jesus Death? Who Is Christ to Them?

Muslims believe in two main theories: that Jesus was never nailed to the cross or that Jesus was nailed to the cross but did not die there. Only one verse in the Quran references and denies the crucifixion of the prophet Jesus. Quran 4:157–158 says:

> That they said (in boast), "We killed Christ Jesus the son of Mary, the Messenger of Allah.;- but they killed him not, nor crucified him, but so it was made to appear to them, and those who differ therein are full of doubts, with no (certain) knowledge, but only conjecture to follow, for of a surety they killed him not:- Nay, Allah raised him up unto Himself; and Allah is Exalted in Power, Wise;- And there is none of the People of the Book but must believe in him before his death; and on the Day of Judgment he will be a witness against them.

Based on the first part of Quran 4:157, Muslims, except for the tiny Ahmadiyya sect, do not believe that Jesus was crucified. The denial of the cross demands a critical analysis from the viewpoint of a bystander. They ask, how can Christians declare that Jesus is the son of God and, in the meantime, believe that God Almighty, in his power, can allow his son to be killed at the hands of the Jews? Is God that weak in the eyes of Christians? This is a serious outrage and sin to Muslims—blasphemy. Their conclusion is that the Christ crucifixion is taboo and not true.

The second theory is that someone like Jesus died on the cross, but it was not actually Jesus of Nazareth. All Muslims agree that, on that fateful day two thousand years ago, someone was placed on the cross and was also killed on the cross. The question is, was that someone Jesus or another person? Whether it was Jesus or not, the word similarity here refers to showing the likeness of death. Since the question here is of the death of Jesus, the likeness of the death of Jesus was shown and the Muslim is already deceived! The following are twelve views Muslims have about Christ's crucifixion.

- The Quran states that Jesus was not killed; neither did he die on the cross (Quran 4:157). In the Muslim's mind, Allah is merciful. He could not allow his prophet and Imam, Jesus, to be crucified by his enemies. For that reason, they believe God saved him and safely took him up to heaven.
- All the prophets of Islam are successful in their message, and for God to allow an ambassador of himself to be crucified would mean that God failed his messenger.
- "Allah is just." He saved Jesus from suffering on the cross, but he let Judas, the betrayer, be crucified instead (Quran 4:157).
- A Roman soldier or guard was made to look like Jesus and was crucified.
- A disciple of Christ volunteered to take Christ's place. The disciple was one who wanted to die instead of Christ because Jesus promised him a place in paradise.
- God put a likeness of Christ on another man who was with Christ. A Jewish bystander was mistakenly crucified instead.
- Some groups say that Jesus took a drug that put him in a coma-like state and that he was later revived in the tomb.
- The Quran teaches that everybody must ask for his own forgiveness from Allah. No human being is able to carry the sins of another person in Allah's judgment (Quran 17:15, 35:18, 39:3, 53:38).
- Allah does not need a mediator or bloody sacrifices, lambs, and substitutes to forgive sins, according to the Quran. God is sovereign; he forgives whom he wants and misleads whom he wants (Quran 6:39, 13:27, 14:4, 16:93, 35:8, 74:31). If Allah seduces someone, no

one can help him anymore (Quran 4:88, 143, 7:178, 186, 13:33, 17:97, 18:7, 39:23, 36, 40:33, 42:44, 46).

Muslims believe their good deeds expel their bad deeds (Quran 11:114). Many Muslims consider themselves good enough to achieve justification by their own capabilities. They hope that they will fulfill all duties according to the Islamic law. They certainly do not believe that evil men can do anything without God's permission!

Allah has determined the destiny of every human being while the individual is still in the mother's womb, and it would be impossible to resist Allah's determination. Nothing would happen in a man's life except what has been written in the original book in heaven about him. Many Muslims think that the cross is only a cover for all kinds of political and religious crusaders who wanted to destroy the power and the culture of the Islamic states.

However, we find from these verses below that the Quran does not deny the actual death of Christ before his ascension: "Peace on me on the day I was born, and on the day I die and on the day I am raised to life" (Quran 19:33); "When Allah said: O Isa! I will cause you to die and ascend you to my presence and clear you of those who disbelieve" (Quran 3:55). "I was among them, but when didst cause me to die, thou art the watcher over them, and thou art witness of all things" (Quran 5:117).

Biblical Arguments about Christ's Crucifixion

The first argument is by proving the Bible's inspiration, truth, morality, and inerrancy. How, then, do we converse with Muslims about the crucifixion? A major stumbling block preventing the Muslim from believing in Christ's redemption is the belief that the Bible was corrupted. Muslims, understandably, point to the hundreds of Bible translations. It is important to direct the Muslim's attention to the fact that the Bible is inspired by God and has not changed. Open your Bible when you share with a Muslim that Christ was crucified. Give an answer from the word of God. Don't just challenge their thinking; give them an exact thought from the scriptures to wrestle with. The Bible is written by God, the Holy Spirit; let them face God's word.

The following are some simple proofs you can use.
Proof #1: The Bible is talking about God himself and is inspired by God and is unchangeable.

- All scripture is God-breathed and is useful for teaching, rebuking, correcting, and training in righteousness (2 Timothy 3:16).
- "Heaven and earth will pass away, but my words will never pass away. (Matthew 24:35, NIV).
- The grass withers and the flowers fall, but the word of our God endures forever (Isaiah 40:8, NIV).

Proof #2: The Quran itself states that the Bible is guidance for all mankind and Muslims are supposed to read it (10:94; 5:46; 3:3).

- "I warn everyone who hears the words of the prophecy of this scroll: If anyone adds anything to them, God will add to that person the plagues described in this scroll. And if anyone takes words away from this scroll of prophecy, God will take away from that person any share in the tree of life and in the Holy City, which are described in this scroll" (Revelation 22:18–19, NIV).
- If God is powerful, almighty, and eternal, as the Muslim believes, then who has the courage and power to face God and change his word? Jesus himself said that scripture cannot be set aside or broken (John 10:35). Attempts may be made, but the truth of the scripture remains the same.
- Because most Muslims believe that the Bible has been corrupted, many missionaries and pastors agree that we should ask Muslims the following questions: Who corrupted the Bible? When was the Bible corrupted? Where was the Bible corrupted? Why was the Bible corrupted? Where is the original Bible? What parts of the Bible were corrupted? Was the Bible corrupted before or after the life of Muhammad? Neither Muslims nor their leaders have complete answers for that.

Proof #3: The solid history of the written Word.

The books of the Old Testament were written from approximately 1400 BC to 400 BC. The books of the New Testament were written from approximately 40 AD to 90 AD. So anywhere between 1,900 and 3,400 years have passed since a book of the Bible was written, and no word have changed. The original Old Testament was written mainly in Hebrew, with some Aramaic, but the original New Testament was written in common Greek. The eyewitnesses to the life of Jesus, including Matthew, Mark, Luke, John, Paul, James, Peter, and Jude, wrote the gospels, letters, and books that became the Bible's New Testament. These authors quote from thirty-nine books of the Old Testament and widely circulated their materials so that, by about 150 AD, early Christians were referring to the entire set of writings as the New Covenant. During the 200s AD, the original writings were translated from Greek into Latin, Coptic (Egypt), and Syriac (Syria) and were widely distributed as "inspired scripture" throughout the Roman Empire and beyond. In 397 AD, in an effort to protect the scriptures from various heresies and other religious movements, the current twenty-seven books of the New Testament were formally and finally confirmed and canonized at the Synod of Carthage. The books of the Bible have been copied again and again. Copies of copies of copies have been made, and the consistency and reliability has been proven over and over by scholars. If we compare these manuscripts with the Bible that in is our hands today, we will see no difference.

Proof #4: The fulfillment of the forty-four Old and New Testament prophecies regarding Christ's death and resurrection:

- The graphic and accurate prediction of Jesus's suffering death in Isaiah 53.
- Jesus repeatedly used and quoted from the Old Testament, "just as Moses lifted up the snake in the desert so must the son of man lifted up" (John 3:14, NIV). Jesus compared himself with the snake; the Son of Man must be lifted up to satisfy God's wrath on behalf of sinners who believe in him, because in his love, (John 3:16) Jesus absorbed the sins of all sinners.

- "God made Him who had no sin to be sin for us, so that in him we might become the righteousness of God" (2 Corinthians 5:21, NIV).

- Jesus emphasized that there is no other possibility of salvation for those who had been led astray by the evil one, except for him dying in their place.

- Jesus shared the purpose of his dying on the cross to Nicodemus (John 3:1–13).

- Jesus predicts why he should die many times to his disciples, and also the reason why he should suffer (Matthew 17:22–23; 20:17–18).

- Jesus's disciples didn't understand until he was resurrected and appeared to them (John 20, 21). If Jesus knew that he would die, why did he not flee abroad or emigrate, like Muhammad, from Mecca to Medina? Why did he not hide or flee to another area? It is clear from scripture that he didn't flee because of the love for and obedience to his father's will. Jesus prayed, "My Father, if it is not possible for this cup to be taken away unless I drink it, may your will be done" (Matthew 26:42, NIV).

The fulfillment of these prophecies guarantees the inspiration of the Bible regarding Jesus's death and resurrection.

Proof #5: The Bible's Uniqueness.
All the authors reflect the same values and message, in spite of their different backgrounds, cultures, and languages. The writers of the Bible are a group of people from the most diverse backgrounds. The Bible is composed of sixty-six books, by about forty different writers of various backgrounds, living during a period of about sixteen hundred years, yet they present one simple message: God, in his love, sent his one and only son, Jesus Christ, to suffer and die on the cross and be resurrected to save and give eternal life to those who believe in him (John 3:16; 1 John 4:8, 16). There is perfect unity between the books of the Bible, covering hundreds of subjects in many fields. Who but God could produce such a book? Such a miracle can only be explained by there being one divine author and his Holy Spirit, who was in control of all these human writers.

This means that what the Bible says is true and has a basic unity of thought and principles that cannot be broken or contradicted.

The Apostle Paul stated that if there was no death, then there is no resurrection, but since the death of Jesus was not questioned, Paul did not have to discuss it in his books in any detail. He mentioned earlier in his letter to the church in Corinth that the center of his message is, "Jesus Christ and him crucified" (1 Corinthians 2:2). Writing about the resurrection, Paul states: "And if Christ has not been raised, our preaching is useless and so is your faith. More than that, we are then found to be false witnesses about God, for we have testified about God that he raised Christ from the dead. But he did not raise him if in fact the dead are not raised. For if the dead are not raised, then Christ has not been raised either. And if Christ has not been raised, your faith is futile; you are still in your sins" (1Corinthians 15:14–17, NIV).

A Second Argument from Genesis 1–3

A central idea behind the first three chapters of Genesis is to present major foundational concepts about the God of Christianity, creation, the origin of sin, and Christ's redemption. If Muslims have a good grasp of the creation account, then they will have a stronger understanding of Jesus's death. Your conversation about these three chapters will lead to a discussion of the core themes of God's love and his solution for humanity. The issue of Christ's death on the cross appears in the first prophesy in Genesis 3:15, NIV: "And I will put enmity between you and the woman, and between your offspring and hers; he will crush your head, and you will strike his heel."

In this passage, God promises to give a seed to the woman and that seed will bruise Satan, even though Satan would bruise His heel. Bruising Jesus's heel is nothing less than His crucifixion and being nailed upon the cross. That same death bruised Jesus's own head. Through his death, Christ won the victory over Satan and redeemed mankind.

A Third Argument from the Fall of Adam

Muslims teach there was no such thing as original sin, rooted in Adam's fall. They believe that each individual will be judged on his or her own merits.

Muslims will not understand Jesus's redemption unless they acknowledge sin and are convinced that they, too, are sinners. They cannot understand God's love until they understand God's wrath, judgment, and hatred of sin. They cannot understand God's grace and mercy to humanity until they realize that humanity needs help. After you have shown that there is an original sin, then you must show that everyone is guilty of it. You must show that there is no human way to be cleansed of this sinful state and that only a perfect and eternal sacrifice for sin can perfectly atone for sin, and that Jesus was Christ, God's Messiah, sent to be that perfect, eternal atonement sacrifice. This is a very tall order for someone who doesn't believe in sin to begin with. I believe it is best to begin from his or her own book. What does the Quran say about Adam's sin? It says: We said: "O Adam! dwell thou and thy wife in the Garden; and eat of the bountiful things therein … Then did Satan make them slip from the (Garden), and get them out of the state (of felicity) in which they had been. We said: "Get ye down, all (ye people) with enmity between yourselves. On earth will be your dwelling place" … Then learnt Adam from his Lord words of inspiration, and his Lord turned toward him, for He is oft-Returning, Most merciful" (Quran 2:35–37).

The Following Are Twelve Types of Sins and Quranic References:

Khati'a خطيئة: A small sin that is unintentional or made by mistake.

Ithm اثم: A deliberate and intentional sin. This type of sin conveys a wrong attitude toward either God or humans.

Haram حرام: Forbidden or prohibited, especially in a religious sense for ritual taboos.

Zanb ذنب: This is the word for sin that is most repeated in the Quran (thirty-nine times). They are confessing that they have mixed a righteous action with an evil action.

Saiyy'a صايعه: A calamitous thing (offense, misdeed), which involves injury to the person who commits it.

Sharr شر: An evil similar to saiyy'a or khati'a in a general sense for all sins. The Quran says in Sura 4:112, "If any one kasaba (earns) a fault or a sin ... he carries a false charge."

Zulm ظلم: It means unfairness or injustice. The Quran says of Adam and Eve, "Or ye run into injustice (harm and transgression)" (2:35).

Wizr وزر: A burden of sin, as in the Quaranic saying, "And removed from thee thy burden, which did gall thy back" (94:2–3).

Kufr كفر: Disbelief, as in 49:7, "Has made hateful to you unbelief, wickedness, and rebellion."

Fasad فساد: Mischief, as in, "When he [a hypocrite] turns his back ... [he] spread mischief through the earth and destroyed crops and cattles [sic]. But God loveth not mischief" (2:205).

Fisq فسق: Moral perversity, as in, "Manifest Sign; and none reject them but those who are perverse" (2:99). The term fisq is used when a person goes beyond that which God has limited for moral behavior.

Su' سوء: Evil or misfortune, as in 4:123, "whoever works evil will be requited accordingly. Nor will he find, besides God, any protector or helper."

There are other sins in Islam, such as killing, committing adultery, stealing, and shirk, which means associating another deity with God. These are considered sins, but there are no other Quranic terms for the concept of sin.

After addressing the sins in the Quran, the next question is about what the Bible says about sin. Most Christians believe that a weak view of sin will always lead to a weak view of salvation. If a person does not identify the problem of the original sin that human beings inherited from our father, Adam, then a person will generally lower any need for Jesus's atonement.

In the Bible, the concept of sin is that of missing the target. Sin also means failing to do what one ought to do. "If you do what is right, will you not be accepted? But if you do not do what is right, sin is crouching at your door; it desires to have you, but you must rule over it." (Genesis 4:7). In Christian thought, sin needs atonement for the remission of the punishment or other effects of sin. The entrance of sin into the world was occasioned through the disobedience of Adam (Romans 5:12); his and Eve's responses to Satan's temptation resulted in the fall (Gen. 3:1–6; Jn. 8:44; 2 Co. 11:3; Eph. 2:2). Rather his inner nature is inclined toward rebellion and disobedience (i.e., sin). Before the fall, man had a perfect will and freedom to choose the right way. Now, all people are bent toward sin. The sin of Adam and Eve spread to the whole of humanity. By the time of Noah, marriage was being trivialized and dishonored (Genesis 6:1–2); ungodly people were corrupted (Genesis 6:2–5); and violence had become a way of life. God decided to punish this sin. The flood represents God's punishment on the people's sin. Noah was honest and lived according to God's laws (Genesis 7). Only Noah and his family believed and entered the ark and were saved (Genesis 6:18). God said there was only one "door," one "ark," and one "promised one" in order to be saved (John 10:9). Noah entered through this door into the ark. The door represents Jesus "I am the gate; whoever enters through me will be saved. He will come in and go out, and find pasture" (John 10:7, 9). After Noah left the ark with his family, he built an altar to the Lord and took every clean bird and offered burnt offerings on the altar (Genesis 8:20–21). Noah offers thanksgiving to God for saving him and his family from the judgment over sin on earth.

When we explain sin to Muslims, we must keep in mind the process of our conversion. Muslims need to recognize that God has made a solution for sin and that this solution is available to them as well. The solution from sin is not self-denial from various comforts and pleasures. It is not a strong will or some good works. The solution is the shedding of the blood of an innocent lamb. The solution to sin is the atonement of Christ through his blood (Romans 3:24). We are saved from the wrath of God through Christ's blood (Romans 5:9). This is why the Bible says, "By His wounds we are healed" (Isaiah 53:5). Not only does God hate sin; he demands that death is the punishment for sin—and not just a physical death, but also a spiritual death that separates the sinner from God. If humanity is evil and ours sin prevents us from having a relationship with

God, how can we ever know or have fellowship with God? As I pointed out earlier, God is holy, and he also loves us. Despite that we are sinners and are condemned to die, he still loves us. And because of his love, he has provided a way for us to have a relationship with him for all of eternity. Christians who work with Muslims use the following two stories as illustrations to help them understand the solution of God through Jesus's atonement.

The first illustration is used when presenting the gospel in order to get the point across that the penalty for breaking the law of God must be paid.

The government or secular laws: Suppose you drive through a red light, and an honest police officer sees you and stops you. He must issue you a ticket because you have broken the law. Even if you say, "Officer, I'm sorry I broke the law," if he's an honest police officer, he will still have to give you a ticket. The law is the law, and there is a penalty for breaking the law! It is the same thing with the law of God.

Islamic laws: In Islam, they do have many form of punishment, and sometimes the death penalty if you break certain laws—as well as other forms of punishment—and they do carry out these punishments whenever they are needed. Muslims say that these laws and punishments are both for our personal as well as the community's benefit.

Christian law: The Bible says that we all have broken God's law. "All have sinned and fall short of the glory of God." The Bible also says that "sin is lawlessness" (1 John 3:4, NIV). The wages for breaking God's law is not a traffic ticket; no, "the wages of sin is death" (Romans 6:23, NIV).

Jewish law: The Torah also says, "We all like sheep have gone astray" (Isaiah 53:6, NIV), and God is recorded as saying, "The heart is deceitful" (Jeremiah 17:9, NIV). The New Testament agrees with this general pronouncement. "For all have sinned and fall short of the glory of God" (Romans 3:23, NIV). Jesus says, "For it is from within, out of a person's hearts, that evil thoughts come ..." (Mark 7:21, NIV). John 2:2, NIV, says, "He is the atoning sacrifice for our sins, and not only for ours but also for the sins of the whole world." Jesus is the savior that King David prophesied about in Psalm 2. Jesus saved us from our sins and took upon himself the punishment for all the sins of the whole world.

The second illustration to your Shi'a Muslim friend is: imagine this. You are standing in an Islamic courtroom for breaking the law, and you are on trial for your life. If you are convicted, you will be sentenced to death. You are led into the courtroom in front of the judge to hear the decision. The judge bangs down his gavel and declares, "You are guilty!" You are sentenced to death. But wait! Something miraculous happens. The judge says, "You are guilty and deserve death. But my son has agreed to be your substitute and will die for you instead. In fact, he has already died, and I will accept his death as payment for your crime. All you must do is to accept what I have said as a fact and believe that your crimes have been paid for and trust me that this is true. If you accept this offer, you will live with my son and me forever. Will you accept this?" What an offer! And if you accept this offer, then not only have your crimes been paid for, but you are totally forgiven and can live with the judge and his son forever. Shi'a don't believe in Imam redemptions. But Jesus redeem us around two thousand years ago. He died for all humanity to free us from our sins, shame, and guilt.

I believe Muslims are aware of sin in their hearts, whether they try to deny it or not. With their lips, they say, "God is great!" but in their hearts, they think, "God is far away! He is silent and doesn't care! No one can know him!" Deep down, even the Muslims know in their hearts that their works are never enough. Fear is in their hearts. They are waiting for someone to tell them the good news.

A Fourth Argument Using the Story of the Sacrifice of Isaac

The Biblical story of Abraham is in Genesis 22:1–14. It illustrates the need for sacrifice to take another's place and gives Muslims a picture of God's sacrifice of his son, Jesus. Verse 1 tells the reader that God was testing Abraham. Muslims believe, in this event, that the son was Ishmael, even though the Quran (37:102–107) does not specify a name.

This story of Abraham is the basis of the New Testament teaching on the atonement, the sacrificial offering of the Lord Jesus on the cross for the sin of mankind (John 8:56). In Genesis 22:1, God called Abraham again by his name, and Abraham heard God's voice. What does this tell us? God speaks and Abraham hears! There was a conversation between God and a human being. Here in this story, God was not tempting Abraham, but testing him. God wants to see if he would do what was right. We read in Hebrews 11:17–19 NIV: "By faith Abraham, when God tested him, offered Isaac as a sacrifice. He who had embraced the promises was about to sacrifice his one and only son, even though God had said to him, 'it is through Isaac that your offspring will be reckoned.'"

Abraham reasoned that God could even raise the dead, and so, in a manner of speaking, he did receive Isaac back from death. In Genesis 22:2–8, God asked Abraham to offer his son as a sacrifice to him. This was an astounding request because Isaac was the son of the promise. "The fire and wood are here," Isaac said, "but where is the lamb for the burnt offering?" Abraham answered, "God himself will provide the lamb for the burnt offering, my son." God uses Abraham's faith as an example to all who came after him as the only means to God (Genesis 15:6; Romans 4:3; 2 Corinthians 5:21, NIV). The actual sacrifice of Isaac and the substitute for him is a picture of Jesus Christ as the Lamb of God, who takes away the sins of the world (John 1:29, NIV).

Christians who believe in Jesus's redemption are descendants of Abraham through their faith in him. The apostle Paul sums it up when he says, "If you belong to Christ then you are the seed of Abraham, and heirs according to the promise" (Galatians 3:29, NIV). There are several common aspects between Isaac and Jesus. Isaac is the promised seed of Abraham. Jesus is the seed of God who brings salvation. Jesus is the Lamb of God without sin, who is innocent (Isaiah 53, John 1:29, NIV). The two sons are related to the promised one, "the only begotten son" (John 1:18, NIV). The two sons are from Abraham's chosen line (Genesis 17:19; Ephesians 1:4–5, NIV). The two sons carried their wood (crosses) on which to die (John 19:17, NIV). The two sons trusted their fathers and obeyed, they did their will (Matthew 26:39; John 19:30; Luke 23:46, NIV). They faced death and experienced resurrection. They got the power and the promises.

The Fifth Argument, Using Six Analogies

The first analogy is the meaning of sacrifice. On the Muslim feast of Al-Adha, at the end of their pilgrimage to Mecca and at the same time in all Islamic countries, Shi'a Muslims slaughter lambs, sheep, rams, or camels, one for each family, to make sure that the blessing of Allah is on them. Within this tradition, blood has significant meanings. The blood is used as protection. When the Shi'a meets to greet their religion's leader, as a sign of showing him support, they say, "We will redeem you with our blood and our spirit." In some villages in the Arab world, blood of animals is offered on the roof of a house as a sign of protecting it from evil. And when someone buys a new car, they kill a lamb as a sacrifice to protect the car. However, most Shi'a Muslims do not know the meaning of the scapegoat in the Old Testament, or about the possibility of a substitute for their sins and the reconciliation by their shed blood (Leviticus 4:4, 14, 24, 33; 16: 6–10). Therefore, it can be helpful for Christians to teach them the laws for sin and burnt offerings noted in the Old Testament and the tradition of the Christian "Good Friday." In this way, they can draw closer to the holy God and understand the purpose of animal sacrifices much better.

The second analogy is the meaning of redemption in both languages, Hebrew and Arabic. In Hebrew, the importance of the blood sacrifices is for salvation. The soul of the animal is in its blood, and when its blood is shed, the soul leaves it. So it was believed that shedding blood for a sacrifice replaces or redeems the soul of the sinner, and he or she thus escapes the punishment he or she deserves. In other words, a person obtains forgiveness of his or her sins. In the Arabic dictionary, it means something like, "Pay for something to save it and then buy it again." And also it means setting a captive free, saving a person from trouble and death by sacrificing oneself.

A third analogy has to do with the six synonymous words in the Quran that describe the creed of sacrifice: *Mansak, Hadi, Adiya, Nahr, Dhabh,* and *Qurban. Adhiya* is an animal sacrifice that takes place at Mecca during the feast of Al-Adha. Ask your Muslim friends about the meaning of sacrifice, and then discuss Jesus as the ultimate sacrifice for mankind. According to Daoud Riad (1996, 98, 99) in his dissertation, the words are:

Mansak (منسك): "To every people did we appoint rites (of sacrifice), that they might celebrate the name of God" (Sura 22:34).

Hadi (هادي): "If ye are prevented (from completing it), send an offering for sacrifice, such as ye may find" (Sura 2:196). When the pilgrim is not able to be there in time for the sacrifice, he or she must send an animal victim to Mecca anyway.

Adhiya (اضحية): This is the word used in Muslim tradition for the animal sacrifice at Mecca. The chief feast is called *'Id al-Adha*, taking its name from the same root.

Nahr (نحر): "Therefore to thy Lord turn in prayer and inhar (sacrifice)" (Sura 108:2). The order here is to the prophet to sacrifice a camel. The meaning of the word *nahr* is to cut the jugular vein, usually used for animal sacrifice.

Dhabh (ضبح): "Forbidden to you (for food) are: dead meat, blood, the flesh of swine … unless ye are able to slaughter it (in due form); that which is sacrificed on stone (altars)" (Sura 5:4). *Dhabh* means to slaughter for sacrificing. The passage gives some Islamic laws that are like Moses' Law (see Leviticus and Deuteronomy). The word is used for Abraham's sacrifice of his son.

Qurban (قربان): "They [also] said: 'God took our promise not to believe in an apostle unless he showed us a sacrifice (Qurban) consumed by fire [from heaven]. Say: There came to you apostles before me, with clear signs and even with what ye asked for. Why then did ye slay them, if ye speak the truth'" (Sura 3:183). In this passage, the Jews are accused of slaying some apostles, but the Quran did not give any examples of this. The word *Qurban* is also used in the following: "Recite to them the truth of the story of the two sons of Adam. Behold! they each presented a sacrifice (to God): It was accepted from one, but not from the other" (Sura 5:30). The Quran did not give the cause of accepting or refusing the sacrifice. The third place in which the word *Qurban* occurs is in Sura 46:28. The meaning is obscure for Zwemer. It is used in this verse for the people who offered sacrifices to other gods, "whom they worshipped as gods, besides God, as a means of access (to God)" (Sura 46:28).

The fourth analogy is the reconciliation, and it is considered a primary principle for approaching Muslims. God initiated reconciliation when he called Adam. "Adam, where are you?" (Genesis 3:9). In 2 Corinthians 5:18, Paul says, "All this is from God who reconciled us to himself through Christ, and gave us the ministry of reconciliation."

A biblical illustration for reconciliation is from Genesis 32, NIV, where Jacob reconciled with his twin brother, Esau, after he deceived him. After long resentment and separation between the two brothers, they finally decided to meet after their father's death. We learn from this story how to approach Shi'a for the purpose of winning them to Christ. Jacob was scared and hesitant about meeting his brother. Esau had the power and was ready to get revenge by killing Jacob because he had deceived him and gotten the blessings from his father, Isaac. Unfortunately, before Jacob approached Esau, God did some work in Jacob's life. God changed Jacob's heart, filled him with his spirit, and broke and humbled him before he approached his brother. I believe Christians should approach Shi'a Muslims in the same way that Jacob approached Esau.

The fifth analogy is the Arabic word *fida'iyeen* فدائين, which means *redeemers*. The term that the West uses is *suicide bombers*, but Shi'a Muslims who commit suicide for the sake of liberating their people and country often call themselves redeemers. Until now, Shi'as encouraged self-sacrifice in fighting enemies and contributing to a spirit of resistance against foreign exploitation and domination. In Shi'a Muslim communities, this resistance is often expressed in the ritualized depiction of the martyrdom of Hussein through passion plays performed during the month of Muharram and at other times of the year. The martyrdom of Hussein in Karbala remains the symbol for freedom, dignity, and the rejection of the tyrants for Shi'a Muslims. Shi'as believe there are some similarities between Jesus Christ and Hussein in that both rejected tyrants and what was wrongful and gave of themselves in the ways of freedom, salvation, dignity, and righteous aspects of life.

Jesus, however, is the true redeemer for Christians. The resurrection is the divine vindication of the fact that Jesus did not die for any crime he had committed, but rather, died in place of sinners needing redemption and justification before an infinitely holy and just God. If it can be proven that Jesus did not die and rise from the dead, then Christianity is nothing more than a great lie that has deceived billions throughout the ages. The Christian is then left without hope, having no assurance of justification and remains in his or her sins (1Corinthians 15:12–19; Romans 4:25, 5:8–11).

The sixth analogy is the redemption of their Imam, Hussein. Passion plays are found in both religions, Christianity and the Shi'a sect. Indeed, Christians and Shi'a are similar in their way of thinking. The passion plays, for Christians, commemorate Jesus's crucifixion and are similar to the Shi'a Muslims performing the horrible murder of Hussein in Karbala. The innocent suffering of Hussein could be used as a good point of connection. Hussein's martyrdom, which supposedly redeemed Shi'a Muslims, is much like Jesus Christ's sacrifice, though we would not hear Shi'a make that comparison. The reason we wouldn't hear of this comparison is because they believe only a Shi'a Imam can suffer and redeem. It needs to be explained to the Shi'a why God chose to save Jesus but Hussein and his followers were left to be decapitated by a Muslim sword.

The Sixth Argument: Using the Quran to Reveal Christ

Much of what the Quran says about Jesus is true, and he is highly respected. If someone studies the Quran, he or she can also find twenty-five names, titles, and attributes of Jesus. Yet nobody knows why Muhammad chose the name of Isa instead of Jesus, since in the Arabic language, *Jesu'a* had been written down from the beginning in the books of the Arabic Christians as the equivalent of *Jesus*. Jesus, in the Quran, is born of a virgin (19:20); born of the Spirit (21:91); raised the dead (3:49); was blessed (19:31); and was holy, sinless, and faultless (19:19). Jesus is Lord (9:31); he is the Messiah (4:171); is the sign to all mankind (19:21, 21:91); is the advocate (39:44); is the word of God (4:171); was raised to heaven (4:158); performed miracles (3:49); creates life; and heal the sick (5:113).

Jesus is the messenger of God in Arabic: Compare Quran 4:169 with John 1:18. Jesus is the truth who reveals God's will to the world. The Quran could not deny the fact that the son of Mary was a man of peace, but in the Quran, Christ is not the son of God; was not crucified; and does not have the power to save or to change humans to be born again. All the titles about the divinity of Christ and of his omnipotence are missing. Shi'a Muslims have five doubt-filled claims about Jesus:

- God is all knowing, but Jesus was not. Jesus is clearly shown to have limitations on his knowledge (Matthew 24:36; Mark 13:32).
- God is all powerful, but Jesus was not. Jesus performed many miracles that he himself admitted were from the power he had derived from God (John 5:19, 5:30).
- God does not have a God, but Jesus did have a God. Jesus acknowledges that there was one whom he worshipped and to whom he prayed and cried out while on the cross (Matthew 27:46; Luke 11:2–4; John 20:17).
- According to the Bible, God is an invisible spirit, but Jesus was flesh and blood. Jesus said that no one had seen or heard God at any time, but his followers both saw and heard his own voice, which is clear proof that Jesus was not God (John 1:18, 4:24, 5:37).
- No one is greater than God, and no one can direct Him—but Jesus acknowledged someone greater than himself whose will was distinct from his own (Luke 18:19, 22:42; John 8:42, 14:28).

One helpful way to approach Muslims is to replace the meaning of the names of Christ from the Bible with the Islamic titles of the son of Mary to explain to the Muslims that the Son of Man is the Son of God as Jesus himself explained it. Whoever reads the Bible can find more than 250 names, titles, and attributes of Jesus. We can explain why all Jesus's titles and names are important and how they apply to Jesus's salvation for us. You can find the names for Jesus in the Bible, like the Lamb of God (John 1:29); the Light of the World (John 8:12); and the Good Shepherd (John 10:11). We can also teach Jesus's stories and parables as illustrations describing how to enter the kingdom of God. Christ established peace between God and men. He loved his enemies. He preferred dying in their place to killing them. Jesus was meek and humble at heart. He never asserted himself by force. He won victory by his faith, love, patience, and hope. Therefore, Shi'a Muslims speak the words, "There is peace on him!" whenever they say his name. They feel that Christ is the true prince of peace. Jesus declared, "My peace I give you. I do not give to you as the world gives. Do not let your hearts be troubled and do not be afraid" (John 14:27, NIV). He can change his followers into peacemakers (Matthew 5:9).

A Seventh Argument Using the Lord's Supper

Christian communion (the Lord's Supper) is the remembrance of Jesus's death and resurrection and the acknowledgement of Jesus Christ's redemption. The cup that we drink from is the new covenant in Jesus's blood, and the bread that we take represents his body and the community that Jesus forms in his suffering. Every time we eat this bread and drink from the cup, we proclaim the Lord's death until he comes (1 Corinthians 11: 23–26, NIV). Shi'a Muslims have an easier time relating to communion than Sunni Muslims.

What are the most important words in any Christian's vocabulary in the Lord's Supper? Perhaps they are *forgiveness* and *church community*. Why did Jesus suffer and die upon the cross? So we could be forgiven! We celebrate this forgiveness in the Lord's Supper every time we participate. Jesus's first words upon the cross were, "Father, forgive them, for they do not know what they are doing" (Luke 23:34, NIV). Jesus prayed this for the scribes and Pharisees who plotted against Him. Jesus prayed this for the crowds that screamed, "Crucify him! Crucify him!" He went to the cross for our sake so we can have good relationships with the Father.

Jesus died on the cross to build his church community around him. By the power of the Holy Spirit, people who believe in his death and resurrection became righteous and pure people so they could testify about Christ to others around them. Then we can love each other as God loves us. This is a powerful message to Shi'a Muslims; as we participated in the Lord's Supper, we've been reminded of the wondrous forgiveness that is ours in Christ, and the sacrificial love of Christ and his followers.

Chapter 4: Understanding Christ's Redemption

Questions for Reflection

1. Does the Quran encourage us to read the Bible?

2. What do Shi'a Muslims believe regarding Jesus's death?

3. Who is Christ is to Shi'a?

4. How do you prove the Bible is not corrupted?

5. How does Shi'a view sin?

6. What is the concept of sin in the Bible?

7. What is the significance to Shi'a of Genesis 22, where Abraham sacrifices Isaac?

8. How do Shi'a view redemptions?

9. Is there any common ideas between Christians and Shi'a?

10. How do you bridge the gap between al-Husain and Jesus's blood sacrifices?

11. Name the seven arguments for Jesus's crucifixion.

PART THREE

The rubber meets the road in this first chapter of the final book. Compelling testimonies are shared in an effort to help the reader understand the eternal impact of NOT sharing the Good News of Christ with Shi'a Muslims. In this current age, no longer can we say, "I never met a Muslim and never had the opportunity". In most cities in the US today, the harvest (for Shia Muslims) is plentiful but the workers are few.

This chapter six encourages the reader to reflect on what they have personally done to share the Gospel and to uncover reasons they might be holding back. We are all called to be the hands and feet of Christ and through the Holy Spirit, we are all qualified.

Seem like a tall order? Perhaps. But what I've just described is what all Christians are called to do. True, there are some who have the gift of evangelism and carry it out with great authority and zeal, but that does not preclude all other believers from sharing their faith until the Good News is shared to the corners of the earth.

A former Shi'a Muslim shared a heartbreaking story with me not so long ago. Mohammad had grown up in a home where Islam wasn't practiced beyond the tradition of celebrating Ramadan and several other Muslim holidays. Growing up, he and his cousin Ali, who grew up in a similar household, were the best of friends. They especially loved to go fishing together and would spend hours and hours on the lake talking and laughing. They were as close as brothers and shared all of their secrets and dreams with each other. By the time they reached their late teen years,

Mohammad's life was starting to take an ugly turn. He was not rooted in beliefs at all, Islamic or otherwise, so when drugs and alcohol were made available to him, he didn't think twice. Soon, he was consumed by these things.

Chapter six, help sharing the Gospel One on One. There are a wide variety of effective evangelical approaches that may be used to bring the Gospel to Shi'a Muslims individually (outside of a corporate church context). The chapter emphasizes that there is no formula, but covers seven approaches that have been found to be effective. Some examples are accompanied by stories and testimonies to bring the scenarios to life for the reader. There are also helpful charts and lists of "Do's and Don'ts" to remind the reader of cultural expectations to help mitigate misunderstandings and to show good will.

Developing a friendship with a Shi'a Muslim doesn't have to be complicated or frightening. Look at the example we have in Jesus. He made an intentional effort to be a friend to all different types of people including Matthew, a tax collector and the Samaritan woman at the well. Being friendly and approachable, along with having a good sense of humor are keys to opening the door to friendship with a Shi'a Muslim. To be friendly is to be a free man who is willing to open his life to others, like Paul in 1 Cor. 9:19-23, "I am free and belong to no man, I make myself a slave to everyone, to win as many as possible…" Like all humans, Shi'a Muslims need to sense real love, not conditional love based upon their response to the Gospel. Shi'a Muslims see Christians as friendly, but not always as good friends. Christians will often have casual contact with them in passing at school, work, social gatherings, stores, etc.… But exchanging simple greetings and pleasantries aren't enough to develop a real friendship.

Chapter seven helps share the Gospel through a Church or Ministry Group. Like the preceding chapter, seven effective corporate church or ministry approaches are covered in this chapter. Having a faith community stand together in agreement on the importance of this common mission can be powerful.

Honestly, it's not so different for any non-believer. Many people, regardless of where they are from, have some ideas and stereotypes about the Church. Some based on their own past experience, or perhaps based on just one or two Christians they know they gave them either a good or bad perception. Some others form opinions based on what they read on social media or what they hear in the media. I know a girl from the same city I live in now who struggled with what she viewed as hypocrisy of Christians. Saying they believe one thing, but doing another thing all together. It was a barrier for her in ultimately accepting the Lord. A wise friend who had witnessed to her finally gave her a very simple truth that opened her eyes and heart. His words to her? "Just because some of us screw it up, doesn't mean the Gospel isn't true".

Since Shi'a Muslims emphasize community, it is important that the Christian group also demonstrate a strong community when witnessing to them. Jesus prayed for his disciples to be united in the world. Shi'a Muslims are a community-oriented race crying out for relationships with others who need love and a sense of belonging. If we consider the life of Jesus Himself, He lived a life of community with his Father and His disciples. Humbly acting in perfect obedience to the Father's will meant that Jesus also lived in fellowship with others. Therefore, a church community should maintain effective communication and develop a structure that will incorporate opportunities for building a natural evangelism with Shi'a Muslims.

Vision and strategy plan for mission and Evangelism among Muslims:

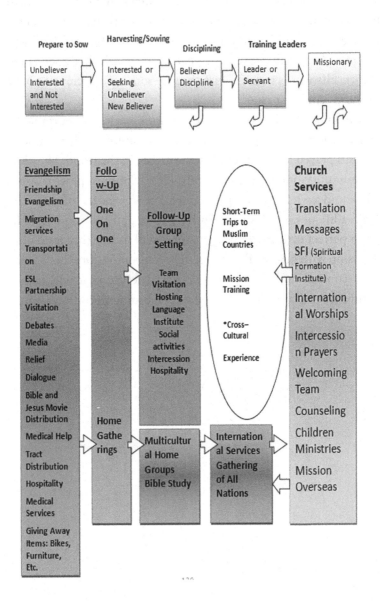

CHAPTER 5
EVANGELIZING TO SHI'A

In this chapter, we will explore a variety of methods that have proven effective in sharing the gospel with Shi'a Muslims. We will share testimonies and stories gathered from different perspectives—from pastors, ministry leaders, Shi'a Muslim converts, and, most importantly, normal believers just like you and me, who are not so "normal" in that they are filled with the power of Christ. Although this topic may seem narrow on the surface, it's critical to remember a few things.

First, there is no formula to evangelize to any particular group. These are merely ideas designed to motivate, encourage, and inspire others. Our God is so much greater than what is written in these books. If you ask and listen, the Holy Spirit will guide each conversation you have with Shi'a Muslims to help you create interactions that are as unique as God created each of us and each of them to be.

Second, although these chapters are focused on reaching out to Shi'a Muslims, as believers, we are called to be ambassadors of the ministry of reconciliation to *all* unbelievers. We believe strongly that many of these methods can be easily leveraged to evangelize to anybody around you who doesn't know Christ. In Milwaukee, where I live, we are so blessed to have a strong immigrant population that consists of people from many different parts of the world. Opportunities are all around; anyone can fulfill a call to the nations without ever leaving their own community.

And finally, just a reminder that *you* are qualified to share the gospel. It's so easy sometimes for Christians to disqualify themselves. "But, I'm a newer believer," "But I don't have any scripture memorized," "But, I don't know anything about Islam!" The list goes on and on. If you are a follower of Christ, you have the Holy Spirit in you and that, alone, qualifies you. Trust God; step out in faith, and see what He will do in and through you to change the world!

Who Is an Evangelist?

> An evangelist is a person with a special gift from the Holy Spirit to announce the Good News of the gospel. The same Greek word that is translated as "gospel," "preaching," and other evangelistic words in the New Testament is used over sixty times in Paul's writing alone. It is verb form, meaning, "to announce the Good News," occurs over fifty times. The Greek word for evangelist means "one who announces the Good News." The word evangelist was apparently rare in the ancient world, but is used three times in the New Testament. It is listed as one of the gifts God has given to the church in Ephesians 4:11. Philip the termed an evangelist (Acts 21:8), and Timothy is charged by Paul to "do the work of an evangelist (2Timothy 4:5). (Graham 1989, 10)

The message the evangelist carries is clear if we read Acts 4:12, NIV: "Salvation is found in no one else, for there is no other name under heaven given to men by which we must be saved." The message of evangelism is all about love. It is about how Jesus Christ, by his suffering, death, and resurrection, became a gospel. Paul, in 1 Corinthians 15:3–4, NIV, makes the message of the gospel clear: "Christ died for our sins according to the scriptures. He was buried … he was raised on the third day … and he appeared to the apostles …" Any message other than the gospel of Jesus Christ is not true evangelism. Evangelism is sharing the truth, the word of God delivered to others, in love.

Who is called to evangelize? This person is someone who has experienced the forgiveness of God and his righteousness (Isaiah 6, NIV); it is someone who has experienced the power of the cross and the resurrection

(John 20, 21, NIV); it is one who has responded to the call of Jesus to "Go to the whole world and preach the gospel ..." (Mark 16:15, NIV); and it is one who has the assurance of his salvation in Christ and can say, "God loves me; the reaction of my experience is to tell others."

To evangelize to Shi'a Muslims, one must demonstrate all the above, but it's especially important that he or she shows the fruits of the Spirit in their lives. They should be able to answer the unique questions that are raised by Shi'a Muslims. Also, evangelists must be someone who has responded to the mission call (John 10:9, NIV). Our Lord, Jesus Christ, says, "As the Father has sent me, I am sending you" (John 20:21, NIV). "How then, can they call on the one in whom they have not believed? And how they can believe in the one of whom they have not heard? How can they hear without someone preaching to them? And how can they preach unless they are sent? As it is written, "How beautiful are the feet of those who bring good news!" (Romans 10: 14–15, NIV). When the prophet Isaiah got the calling to share God's word with his people, he saw God's holiness and power in a vision. Isaiah also saw his own wickedness, and he acknowledged that no one could go to share the gospel in his or her own strength. God changed and purified him; then the question came to him, "Whom shall I send, and who will go for us?" And then Isaiah said, "Here am I! Send me." And God said, "Go and tell these people."

In the end, the evangelist will not be intimidated by Islam, crowds, or anti-Christian authorities. His or her passion for the gospel is such that they will not be deterred, even if the authorities forbid the proclamation of the gospel (Acts 5:27–28, 5:40–42, NIV). And they will not be afraid to confront sin, boldly warning others of its consequences.

Does this seem like a tall order? Perhaps, but what I've just described is what all Christians are called to do. True, there are some who have the gift of evangelism and carry it out with great authority and zeal; but that does not preclude all other believers from sharing their faith until the good news is shared to the corners of the earth.

A former Shi'a Muslim shared a heartbreaking story with me not so long ago. Mohammad had grown up in a home where Islam wasn't practiced beyond the tradition of celebrating Ramadan and several other Muslim holidays. Growing up, he and his cousin Ali, who grew up in a similar household, were the best of friends. They especially loved to go fishing together and would spend hours on the lake, talking and laughing. They were as close as brothers and shared all their secrets and dreams with each other.

By the time they reached their late teen years, Mohammad's life was starting to take an ugly turn. He was not rooted in beliefs at all, Islamic or otherwise, and so when drugs and alcohol were made available to him, he didn't think twice about using them. Soon, he was consumed by these things.

Meanwhile, Ali had met a girl and was engaged to be married. Mohammad was excited. Weddings are huge, multiday events where he is from, filled with delicious foods, drinks, and dancing until the wee hours of the morning. Ali's wedding proved to be all these things and more. It was truly a joyous occasion and a much-welcome break from a lifestyle that was lonely and exhausting for Mohammad.

In the early morning light, Ali and his new bride sped off from the wedding venue in a fancy sports car, as is tradition. Moments later, there was a crash. Ali died senselessly, leaving behind a grieving young widow and hundreds of shocked wedding guests. It would be one of the darkest days in Mohammad's life, one that plunged him even deeper into his reckless habits.

Years went on, and Mohammad's life spiraled downward. He reached a point where he did not care whether he lived or died. He took crazy chances, picked fights with dangerous people, and, every day, tempted fate. He came close to dying several times, but each time, God somehow showed up and saved him even though he did not recognize that until years later.

When he was in his thirties, something miraculous happened. First, his mom was saved through a Christian satellite TV program. Then his sister. Then his father. They began to pray for Mohammad's salvation daily. Although he saw the changes in his family and couldn't deny that this was a good thing, he continued to reject the gospel. But a few years later, after he had reached rock bottom and was truly in a life-or-death situation, Mohammad surrendered his life to the Lord. Today, he is a completely new creation in Christ and lives to serve him. He has a light and joy in him that he never had before. Yet, sometimes his eyes well up with tears as he remembers Ali. His first best friend whom he would have given his life for. He grieves not only for his cousin's short life, but for his eternal life. If only someone would have shared the gospel with him. If only he had known the truth and had had a chance to accept Jesus before he died. If only Mohammad had been saved first and could have told him. But no one had told Mohammad either, as he was busy wasting his time with drugs and alcohol for so many lost years.

The world is waiting for you. People are waiting for you. They are not waiting for someone with a special gift, someone with the "perfect words," or someone who has memorized the Bible. They are waiting for all of us who know and proclaim the truth of Christ to simply tell them so that they may hear, believe, and have eternal life.

Chapter 5: Evangelizing to Shi'a
Questions for Reflection

1. When you think about the work of an evangelist, what are some things that come to your mind?

2. Do you know anyone who you would consider to be an effective evangelist? Why would you say he or she is an evangelist?

3. Think of three things you have done in the last month to share the gospel with others through your words or actions. If you have not done this, think of three things you would like to do in the next month to share the gospel. Write them down. Spend time in prayer, asking God for guidance and wisdom to show you opportunities.

4. What is your biggest hesitation in sharing the gospel with others? Are there specific ways you have been able to push past this and be obedient? If so, what was the outcome?

5. When did you first hear the gospel? Who shared with you? What did he or she say?

6. Have you ever been asked to share your testimony? What did you share? If you haven't, what do you think you would share with others?

7. Have you ever had a cultural misunderstanding in travel or when dealing with someone locally from another country? Share with the group. What was your reaction? What did you learn from it?

8. When you came to the Lord, what were some of the questions you had initially? What topics required study and conversation to truly understand them?

9. What biblical verses have you memorized? What specific methods did you use to commit these verses to memory?

10. Have you ever been asked a particularly difficult question about your faith and why you believe what you believe? What was the question? How did you respond?

11. How can we build bridges with Muslims?

CHAPTER 6

SHARING THE GOSPEL, ONE ON ONE

The issues preventing Shi'a Muslims from accepting the truth of the gospel are multifaceted and complex. But at the core, it's a spiritual problem—one that can be remedied only with a changing of hearts and minds through the power of Christ.

There are a wide variety of effective evangelical approaches that may be used to bring the gospel to Shi'a Muslims. You will need to determine which of these might work best for you and which are most aligned with your spiritual gifts. And always remember that one size does not fit all. Seek the Lord for guidance, and he will show you what's best in every situation and with every person.

I am overviewing seven approaches that I have personally found to be effective in reaching out to Shi'a Muslims one on one. In this chapter, I will share additional approaches that I have personally found to be effective through group, church, or ministry efforts.

Seven Ways to Evangelize to Shi'a Muslims One on One

1) Extend friendship.
Developing a friendship with a Shi'a Muslim doesn't have to be complicated or frightening. Look at the example we have in Jesus. He made an intentional effort to be friends with all different types of people, including

Matthew, a tax collector, and the Samaritan woman at the well. Being friendly and approachable, along with having a good sense of humor, are keys to opening the door to friendship with a Shi'a Muslim. To be friendly is to be a free person who is willing to open his or her life to others, like Paul did in 1 Corinthians. 9:19–23, NIV: "I am free and belong to no man, I make myself a slave to everyone, to win as many as possible …" Like all humans, Shi'a Muslims need to sense real love, not conditional love based upon their responses to the gospel. Shi'a Muslims see Christians as friendly, but not always as good friends. Christians will often have casual contact with them at school, work, social gatherings, and stores, but exchanging simple greetings and pleasantries aren't enough to develop a real friendship.

I will share seven strategies to help develop and strengthen friendships with Shi'a Muslims below:

The first strategy is to be intentional in casual contact with Shi'a Muslims. Developing an acquaintance isn't the objective, but it's a starting point. Be aware of those around you who look different, dress different, or speak in a different language. Approach them with a cheerful spirit and a friendly smile. Remember a person's name, and then greet him or her by that name the next time. Ask people appropriate questions that reflect interest and acceptance. Generally, people enjoy being asked about themselves, especially in our busy society today when people don't always stop to get to know one another. Many Shi'a Muslims are likely proud of their heritage and culture and will be delighted to share with someone who seems genuinely interested. Be a good listener and, even if you disagree with something, remind yourself of the interest God has in their lives and of how he loves them.

If your acquaintances are new to the country, inquire not only about where they are from, but also ask them their impressions of life in the United States or in your city. Inquire to see if they have any questions. Our culture and traditions might feel as different and strange to them as theirs do to you. Conversations open the doors to understanding, and you may very well find, as they might, that the origins of some traditions are quite beautiful, making them not quite so strange after all. Focus on positive aspects of Christianity and western culture, but don't be afraid to tackle tough questions should they arise. We aren't perfect either, and it's okay to admit that.

The second strategy is being available to and for them. Sharing your time and meals with new friends or calling them periodically will certainly help a friendship to grow. Although sharing faith is important, it cannot be the sole purpose of your interactions or conversations. Nobody wants to feel like a project, but everyone wants to be loved and accepted. If you are not verbally sharing the gospel, as a believer carrying the Holy Spirit inside you, your faith will be evident in all you say and do. They will notice something is different about you. Avoid political and patriotic arguments. We Christians need to learn to stay away from intellectual arguments and speak to the heart more than the mind by showing them the practical love of Christ. Someone I know once said, "When you share your story with your Muslims friend, make sure that you talk to his heart before you talk to his mind. Eventually, his heart will explain it to his mind." That is true for the Shi'a Muslim as well.

Remember that even moderate or nonpracticing Shi'a Muslims are likely to get defensive if they feel their faith and culture, which are so often tightly intertwined, are being attacked. There are certain "truths" that have been ingrained in them since birth and, even if they don't feel passionately about these things, if they perceive that you are not respecting their culture or religion, you will likely be met with an argument. For example, most Shi'a Muslims believe that the United States and the power of Zionism pit the West against the Islamic world. Radical Shi'a Muslims believe that Christians and Jews partners with the West in a war against Islam, including the Shi'a Muslim world. Do not attempt to defend the crusades and the Christian views that fueled them. Every educated Shi'a Muslim remembers that it was the popes in Rome who called for crusades against Islam in the past. Be wise when you quote the Old Testament. Your Muslim Shi'a friend may think that you share the gospel solely as a defense of Israel, so be sensitive about what you are sharing and when. We know that Shi'a Muslims do not distinguish between Christianity and Americans. Christians of any nationality must be careful not to confuse Christ with patriotism and pride of country.

The third strategy is about asking questions that could be helpful to initiate deeper conversations with your Shi'a friend, such as the following:

- "I'm interested in what Shi'a Muslims think about God. I would like to know your opinion. Can we have coffee sometime to discuss?"
- "I'm interested in getting to know more about your beliefs and culture. It's such a wonderful opportunity to have a friend with such a different background who can share these things firsthand with me."
- "I know that you are interested in learning as much as you can about Christians and American life while you are here in the United States. I would love to have the opportunity to share with you just what it means to me."
- "There have been many misconceptions about Christianity, and maybe you'd like to know why we believe what we do. I'd love to share with you and maybe, if you wanted, you could share with me your experiences along this line too."
- "I'm interested in learning more about your country and your culture. Tell me more about these things. What is traditional food like there? Tell me about how you celebrate holidays."
- Ask to see any photographs of your Shi'a friend's life, home, family, and so on.
- Share your own life and your family's photographs. Ask questions like, how large is your family? What is your position of birth order?
- Refer to a map and ask where your friend's home is located. Discuss the environment in the Middle East.
- "What kinds of work do you do or, in general, do men and women do in your home country? Do married women work outside the home? If not, why? What about the husband's responsibility at home? Do women hold political office in your home country?"
- "What are Shi'a wedding customs like in your home country?"
- "How do you feel about the role women play in North American culture? How do you feel about equality for men and women?"

The fourth strategy is essential, and that is praying daily for your Shi'a Muslim friend and keeping in contact with him or her—not just via email or phone, but also by seeing him or her in person once or twice a month. Remember his or her birthday by sending a card or planning a party. Invite your friend to participate in your personal celebrations, including birthdays, holidays, and special events. Plan places to go together like athletic events, trips out of town, concerts, lakes, parks, shopping, and museums. Plan to spend time together doing recreational activities like soccer, tennis, kite-flying, volleyball, and basketball. The possibilities are endless, and, through these activities, you may find that you have much more in common than you ever imagined.

The fifth strategy is to go deeper in your friendship by being sincere and genuine when you share your faith. The deeper a friendship, the more you have earned respect and trust and thus, opportunities to speak truth into someone's life. Although we should use wisdom and discernment with what we share and when, do not be apologetic about or ashamed of your faith. It's one thing to share what you feel or believe and quite another thing to hit someone over the head with it, relentlessly trying to convince him or her to believe or feel the same. Avoid the latter, but when you are sharing your heart with someone, it's much more difficult to offend or have someone argue with you even if he or she doesn't agree. Your feelings are your feelings, after all. Be sure that your friend leaves the discussion knowing that you like him or her for who he or she is and not the person's beliefs. I need for the other person to acknowledge the fact that I am here and that I am a person who deserves to be loved and trusted. I want someone to feel that I am worth recognizing.

The sixth strategy is about learning their interests and discovering their gifts and skills. Learn about the hopes and desires they have for their lives. Show interest and concern if they share problems with you. Be honest about yourself and acknowledge your faults to them when appropriate. It's important for them to know that Christians struggle just like everyone else and are far from perfect (for if we were perfect, we would not need a savior in Jesus Christ). Sharing with your friends about an issue or something you are working on improving in your own life could present a wonderful opportunity to talk about how your faith is helping you in this area, or to share about God's forgiveness and grace when we repent. Share Jesus's incarnation and love (John 3:16; Philippians 2:5–8, NIV), and about how God feels for his lost children. Share the story of the prodigal son or tell them why Jesus had to suffer and die for our sins. Encourage your friend to learn more about Christianity and about the purpose of Jesus death and resurrection if they seem interested or want ask questions, but always offer to help them learn more through subsequent conversations, books, or movies.

The seventh strategy is to give time and commitment generously to your Shi'a Muslim friend as opportunities arise. Time is not always for yourself and for your priorities. In Matthew 4:17, we read that the time had come for Jesus to preach, and in Matthew 16:21, the time had come to explain his suffering, death, and resurrection. In both instances, the time stressed in these texts does not refer to a schedule, but rather to an opportunity. You must be willing to sacrifice your time and follow as God leads where he is at work at any given time. This means walking not according to your own timeline, but rather, in accordance to God's. Our model should be to do as Jesus did: "Jesus gave (the Jews) this answer: 'I tell you the truth, the Son can do nothing by himself; he can do only what he sees his Father doing, because whatever the Father does the Son also does'" (John 5:19, NIV).

A Quick Word on Cultural Differences

Our cultural differences make life so much richer and more interesting. But sometimes, when we simply don't know what we don't know about these differences, we can unintentionally offend or hurt our new friends.

I have a friend who is a former Shi'a Muslim and who is now a strong, practicing Christian. He is kind and forgiving, but even so, he has forty years of Shi'a culture and tradition in him. Sometimes, he finds that he is surprised at what hurts or offends him until he stops to think about intentions and culture differences. For example, he has American friends who hosted a Thanksgiving dinner for their immediate family. The day after Thanksgiving, he was invited to their home for fellowship and dessert. When a delightful pumpkin pie was presented, they laughed and told him it was left over from their feast the day prior, and would he like a slice? He was immediately offended and sharply declined it. In his home country, serving anyone outside of immediate family food intended for others or that had been prepared for another meal the day prior is a grave insult. Most Shi'a feel this shows great disrespect, and one would not even feed this to a dog, much less a friend. By comparison, in our culture, we probably wouldn't think twice about this and would happily accept it, laughing with our friends about how much is prepared for Thanksgiving that people can't possibly finish.

The deeper the friendship, the less likely this is to happen, even if your behavior hurts them because they will know your heart and your intentions. Don't overthink things, but remember that our actions, although sometimes small, can have unintended consequences.

Shi'a Muslim Cultural Expectations versus Christian Responses

Shi'a Muslim Expectation	Christians	Muslim Feelings
Expected to shake hands (Shi'a women usually don't shake hands with strange men, for example)	You didn't	You don't like me/you don't know my culture
Expected to be respected	You didn't	You think you are better
Expected to talk with me	You didn't	You don't like me and my family, or maybe you don't think I look good
Expected to be my friend	You only say hello and good-bye	You don't like Muslims
Expected to meet my need	You avoid me	I did something wrong
Expected language help	You didn't	You assume I know English
Expected to spend time talking and enjoying each other's company	You are serious	You don't enjoy my presence
Expected to visit my house	No time	I am not important to you

2) Develop a Christian attitude.

We should not jump to seek out opportunities to build relationships with Shi'a before we build Jesus's attitude in our lives with respect to how we view others. "Your attitude should be the same as that of Christ Jesus" (Philippians 2:5, NIV). Ask yourself before engaging, "Am I helping them? Do I like them? How do I regard them? Are they my enemies? Am I accepting them as people as Jesus did?" "Therefore, since Christ suffered in his body, arm yourselves also with the same attitude" (1 Peter 4:1, NIV). Our attitudes toward Shi'a Muslims and those who are not like us should change. The question that I usually ask in my class when I teach how to evangelize to Muslims is, "What word comes first to your mind when I say *Muslims?*" Most responses are negative, such as, "They're terrorists, bloody people, killers, enemies, wear veils, ignorance, desert, oil, money," and more. When you hear that, you know that none of these Christians will be able to share Christ effectively with a single Shi'a Muslim until their perspectives change. Not all Muslims are the same, and they are not all terrorists. A biblical example can be found in Luke 9:51–55. When Jesus decided to visit the Samaritan villages, he sent messengers on ahead to get things ready for him; but the Samaritan people there did not welcome him. They rejected him because he was heading to Jerusalem. Samaritans are enemies of the Jews. The first reaction that James and John had was that of anger. "Well, these are our enemies anyway, let's kill them all," they said. They wanted to retaliate by calling down fire from heaven on the Samaritans just as Elijah had done to the servants of a wicked king of Israel (2 Kings 1:10, 12, NIV). They didn't want to shake the dust from their feet (Luke 9:5, NIV). But Jesus rebuked his disciples. When a Shi'a rejects us, we also may feel like retaliating, but we must remember that judgment belongs to God.

Christian Attitude—a Short List of "Do's" and "Do Not's"
Do's
1. Be enthusiastic and positive about your faith.
2. Create an environment of acceptance among your Shi'a friends.
3. Be sensitive and deal with them personally; not by their culture and beliefs.
4. Be a wise listener and be trustworthy.
5. Be hospitable and willing to learn.
6. Seek and you will identify many positive things about Shi'a Muslims.
7. Be alert and read your Shi'a Muslim friend's words and behaviors.
8. Remember, in the end, to smile, smile, and then smile some more.

Do Not's

1. Reach out with an envious spirit.
2. Judge all Shi'a Muslims because you have some difficulty understanding Islam or because you have had a bad experience with someone from the Muslim world.
3. Talk down to Shi'a Muslim friends instead of treating them as equals.
4. Measure their culture by the standards or values of your own culture.
5. Think your culture's ways of making friends is the only acceptable way.
6. Assume people from Muslim cultures cannot be fully trusted.
7. Gossip because it causes hard feelings and brings division (Proverb 16:28, NIV)
8. Be afraid of making mistakes. Use mistakes as learning opportunities. give up!

3) Be biblical.

Many of us struggle with memorizing scripture. We know the word; we have read it, and we know God's character and the details of Jesus's life, death, and resurrection through it. But when we are called on to quote it, many of us find ourselves flipping through the Bible to the place where we are "pretty sure" the right verse resides, and we certainly don't have it committed to memory. Memorizing biblical verses can be challenging, but it is helpful and is possible with the help of the Holy Spirit. Consider starting with key verses about salvation to share with your Shi'a friends, including:

o "But to all who did receive him, who believed in his name, he gave the right to become children of God (John 1:12, NIV).
o "For God so loved the world, that he gave his only Son, that whoever believes in him should not perish but have eternal life. For God did not send his Son into the world to condemn the world, but in order that the world might be saved through him" (John 3:16–17, NIV).

- o "Jesus said, I am the way, and the truth, and the life. No one comes to the Father except through me." (John 14:6, NIV).
- o "Therefore, my friends, I want you to know that through Jesus the forgiveness of sins is proclaimed to you. Through him everyone who believes is set free from every sin, a justification you were not able to obtain under the law of Moses." (Acts 13:38–39, Romans 1:16, NIV).
- o "For I am not ashamed of the gospel, for it is the power of God for salvation to everyone who believes, to the Jew first and also to the Greek" (Romans 1:16, NIV).
- o "For all have sinned and fall short of the glory of God" (Romans 3:23, NIV).
- o "For the wages of sin is death, but the free gift of God is eternal life in Christ Jesus our Lord" (Romans 6:23, NIV).

Acknowledge that your Shi'a friends have likely memorized many verses from the Qur'an, if not the entire Qur'an, as part of their education. Given this fact, equipping yourself with scripture will help you to have a solid biblical ground on which to stand. Know your Bible well—more than any other book that sits on your shelf. Don't just seek to memorize, but also to internalize and understand. Your Shi'a Muslim friend may quote the Qur'an from memory, but often this is done without true understanding. When you read or recite the word of God, it will speak for itself. Don't ever use the Bible simply to find texts to prove that your Shi'a Muslim friend is wrong. The word of God is the flood that God has provided for our souls.

Offer a Shi'a Muslim a New Testament with respect, or a Jesus movie or a Christian book as a gift, if the person shows interest in learning more. This is a starting point. When a Shi'a Muslim believes in the Bible, then accepting what it teaches becomes natural, even the difficult parts that might be initially challenging to reconcile against their former beliefs.

4) Build a defensive strategy.

Jesus was a persuasive teacher. He used illustrations in his preaching when he spoke of salvation and the kingdom of heaven. He used logic and gave illustrations from nature, books, history, and everyday incidents. Have an objective to help and encourage your Shi'a Muslim friend by stimulating his or her imagination. In this way, you throw light upon the darkness of Islam. The power of persuasion increases when you intimately know your Shi'a Muslim friends; and, as we have discussed, knowing them comes from actively listening to their opinions and needs. The three projecting ways of defining evangelism in the church can be labeled as presence, proclamation, and convict.

God likes those who use their minds and those who invent things. "Human beings are the most intelligent of God's creatures and have a creative power" (Genesis 1:27–28, NIV). One of God's own characteristics is creativity. Be creative and flexible, and search for new ways to share the gospel with your Muslim friends (Matthew 10:16, NIV). But always continue to equip yourself along the way with the sword of the truth—the Bible.

In sharing the gospel, Christians must also learn how to defend their beliefs from a solid and strong place, in addition to being creative. We need to know why we believe what we believe and not simply parrot what we have been taught from the pulpit. Prove to your Shi'a Muslim friends that your Bible is uncorrupt and has not been changed (1 Peter 3:15, NIV). Prove that Jesus had to die on the cross in order to save human beings from sin. Prove to your friends that Jesus came to build his church and that you are part of his church. Be ready to give logical evidence to the difficult questions about your faith. For example, why are there four gospels rather than just one? Some Muslims argue that Islam has one Qur'an, although Christians have four gospels. So why are there four gospels rather than just one? Perhaps you've never thought about it, but from an outside perspective, it's a fair question. The four gospels are not divergent accounts, but rather the same story of Jesus told from four different viewpoints. All the authors agree concerning the basic life and teachings of Jesus Christ and do not contradict each other, but perhaps emphasize different aspects based upon the authors' personal experiences. In the days of Christ in the Middle East, regions were under the influence of the Greek civilization and Jewish law. The Greek jury system required two or three witnesses before a judge would have a case tried before him. Similarly, God has given us four witnesses, all of whom agree concerning the events of the life of Christ. "Every matter must be established by the testimony of two or three witnesses" (2 Corinthians 13:1, NIV).

Questions like this will arise as you share your faith with others. As we continue to grow in our own faith, we will have more and more answers. However, if you don't know the answer to a difficult question raised by your Shi'a Muslim friend, don't panic. It's perfectly acceptable to say, "You know, that's a great question. I'd love to look into that and then respond." In the process, you will have time to seek wise counsel, pray, and research before delivering an appropriate and accurate answer. Admitting you don't know everything does not compromise your credibility, but rather, it shows humility and a willingness to learn.

5) Build an offensive strategy.

Satan is a key player in our evangelistic efforts because one of his strategies is to keep people from hearing and understanding the gospel. Satan blinds the minds of people. "The god of this age has blinded the minds of unbelievers, so that they cannot see the light of the gospel that displays the glory of Christ, who is the image of God." (2 Corinthians 4:4, NIV). As Christians, we face opposition by Satan and his forces on all sides. God is greater, and the victory is ours through Christ, but let us not underestimate the strategies of Satan. He uses every kind of deception, force, and error to try to destroy the effectiveness of the gospel. Why do Shi'a extremist groups like Hezbollah commit terrible acts of violence? Satan has blinded the minds of the Shi'a Muslims by cutting them off from the truth of who Jesus is and what he has done for them. But because of God, even the most radical of Muslim terrorists can be changed by Christ. Yes, it is true! Sometimes we fall into the trap of thinking that certain people, such as terrorists, are beyond hope. They are so evil that they can never experience spiritual regeneration. But Jesus Christ specializes in changing the hearts of *All* people. Christ can change some of the hardest, most evil people in the world. The apostle Paul was a violent man until the living Christ met him and changed his heart!

So what we need when we evangelize is encouragement from the word through stories of God using men and women who have been filled and anointed by the Holy Spirit and who have the boldness to proclaim the truth. "The weapons we fight with are not the weapons of the world. On the contrary, they have divine power to demolish strongholds" (2 Corinthians 10:4). These "fortresses" are the various forms of pressure that

Satan puts on people to blind them and to keep them in spiritual bondage. The "weapons" that we fight with are not guns or other instruments of violence. Instead, they are spiritual weapons that have the power of God behind them! Some of our spiritual weapons are defensive and enable us to take a firm stand against the flaming darts of Satan (see Ephesians 6:10–17). But the weapons here are offensive. Let me suggest that prayer and courageous evangelism two of the most important offensive weapons in our arsenal.

We can make a huge difference by praying for Muslim nations and for the individuals in them. In fact, when fear begins to grip your mind, stop and pray for Muslims (even those who promote terrorism!). Pray that Muslims would have open hearts and for the gospel to reach them. Ask God to raise up workers to help evangelize to Muslim countries. Pray for those who are already doing this (Ephesians 6:19–20). Jesus Christ is the only answer. Spiritual warfare is necessary in reaching out to the Shi'a. Spiritual warfare is pulling down the dominion of darkness and building the kingdom of God. It includes personal protection using the armor of God, plus intercession to see Shi'a Muslims become responsive to the gospel and be set free (2 Corinthians 10:3–5). You need to be aware that Jesus has defeated Satan and the evil spirits once and for all. And "For our struggle is not against flesh and blood, but against the rulers, against the authorities, against the powers of this dark world and against the spiritual forces of evil in the heavenly realms" (Ephesians 6:12). Distinguish between your Shi'a Muslim friend and the spirit of Islam, which works behind the scenes. The spirit of Islam is the same as the anti-Christ that is described in the Bible. It is a misleading spirit (Genesis 3:1–4); it is savage (Genesis 16:12, Galatians 4:29); it spoils the way of God (Acts 13:10); it disfigures the image of God; it ridicules (Genesis 21:9–10); (Colossians 2:16); it is a lustful, glutinous spirit (Genesis 25:31); it is aggressive, violent, and hypocritical (1 Samuel 15:3–11); and it is one of the spirits of the anti-Christ (1 John 2:18, 4:1–2).

Second, trust God to use you to reach them with a loving, courageous witness. Our courage is expressed best when we face the spirit of Islam. You need to shake the ground under the feet of the Shi'a Muslim, and that means challenging their faith by asking them questions that creates doubt about Muhammad, the Qur'an, and their religion. God's authority is committed to his disciples, and he calls on us to exercise it. Jesus gave his authority to his disciples to deliver people from the devil's authority (Luke 9:1–2, 6; 10:19; Matthew 28:18–20; Mark 16:17–20, NIV). We observe God's authority and power exercised through his people in the Bible (Romans 16:20; Ephesians 6:10–18; James 4:7; 1 Peter 5:8–9, NIV). Moses parted the Red Sea (Exodus 14:1, NIV). Elijah parted the water in the Jordon River (2 Kings 2:7–8, NIV); and Elisha prayed blindness upon the enemy (2 Kings 6:17–18, NIV). Paul pronounced blindness upon Elymas, the sorcerer (Acts 13:11, NIV). Peter pronounced the death of Ananias and Saphirra (Acts 5, NIV). Acts 1:8 speaks of the promise of the power from the Holy Spirit to witness.

Some Shi'a Muslims use magic and witchcraft, and some are possessed with evil spirits. It is especially necessary to exercise Jesus's authority among these Shi'a to free them from these strongholds. Many Christians are fearful of engaging the enemy on the higher levels. Remember that your authority is rooted in your faith in Jesus Christ (Matthew 16:16, 18–19, NIV) and in your unity of belief and purpose (Matthew 18:19, NIV). When your Shi'a Muslim friend gets sick or is in dire need of something, use your faith in Jesus and pray *for* him or her. But also ask if you can pray *with* this person. Explain to your friend that you will be praying to God, in Jesus's name. Share the biblical verses that support this. Generally, Shi'a are open to prayer and discussions about prayer. When Jesus had received all authority from his Father, he commanded his disciples to stand up and to use their authority in Christ to free people from evil spirits and sin and to heal them from their sicknesses. When Jesus's disciples, the seventy-two, returned from their mission, they were overjoyed because they saw God's power with them (Luke 10: 17–18, NIV). In the end, we need to remember that the battle is the Lord's. We are to obey, and he will direct us to the battle, but the victory always belongs to him.

The following is a list of recommendations to remind Christians of their authority when challenging Muslim beliefs:

Do

1. Allow the power of the Holy Spirit to touch the weaker areas in your life (1 John 1:9, NIV).
2. Be clean and prepare to do good works and consecrate yourself (Joshua 3:5; 1 Timothy 2:21, NIV).

3. Be holy and ready for God's move and miracles (Joshua 1, NIV).

4. Dismiss the fear of Islam from your heart.

5. Be strict and stand very strongly on your faith and practice what you speak.

6. Remember that Jesus delivered you from the fear of people, loneliness, darkness, poverty, responsibility, injustice, persecution, future, and death.

7. Rely upon our position of victory in Christ.

Do Not

1. Apologize for believing in Christ.

2. Allow the devil to take ground in your life by leading you to sin. If you do sin, confess and repent quickly (1 John 1:9, NIV).

3. Beat around the bush, but do present your belief in Christ (Matthew10:26–33; Philippians 1:14–15, NIV).

4. Be hesitant to share your story with Jesus.

5. Be timid to present a biblical point of view on the issue (2 Timothy 1:7, NIV).

6. Be afraid to challenge Shi'a and ask them difficult questions about their religion.

7. Doubt the power of your weapon in facing your spiritual enemies (Ephesians 6:10–18; 2 Corinthians 10:3–6; Revelation 11:10–12, NIV).

6) Finding common ground.

There are tremendous barriers between Shi'a Muslim and Christian cultures. These differences cover the realm of relationships, values, ideas about the future, business, families, languages, authority, gender roles, money, priorities, history, conflict solving, religion, food, concerns, age, time, observations, communication, and friendships.

Whenever we are dealing with two or more cultures in evangelism, including our own, we are engaging in cross-cultural ministry. *Culture* is beliefs and methods of meanings and values that shape one's behavior. To be a cross-cultural evangelist to the Shi'a, you need to maintain integrity and perspective as well as be genuine. You should expose yourself to Shi'a culture and make the shifts and adjustments necessary to communicate effectively and to be sensitive to their perspectives and viewpoints.

You must be willing to accept and learn from them. For centuries, Muslims and Christians have stood on separate hills and shouted across the valley at each other, never daring to come together closely enough to truly examine each other's beliefs and answer each other's questions—never truly listen to each other's heartbeat. The fact is, there is a wall-a deep gulf that must be bridged by love and understanding.

So how can we establish common ground? All you need to know is your message and enough about the culture of Shi'a Muslims to help bridge the gap. Shi'a Muslim culture isn't "wrong"; it's just "different" from Christian culture. The table below explains some the differences between North American Christian, Shi'a Muslim and Biblical cultures.

Themes	North American Christian Culture	Arab Shi'a Muslim Culture	The Bible Culture
Relationships	Individualism Independent	Family oriented/ dependent	Love/Community Oriented/respectful
Values	Doing	Being	People
Future	Highly organize/ Strategy plan	Fate, unstructured	Eternity with or without God
Business	Task oriented	Cooperative	Faithfulness
Family	Distant	rooted	Image of God
Authority	Equal/democratic	Hierarchy dominant	Submission in love
Gender roles	Diversity/struggle	Male dominated	Diverse in unity
Money	Idol/resource to achieve dream	Control, position	Our treasure in heaven
Priority	Technology/ paying my bills	Friendship/ spiritualism	Kingdom of God
History	Influence decision	Proud	God speaks thru it
Religion	Freedom of choice	Society choice	Law
Conflict solved	Agencies/Courts	Tribe, family clique	Blood of Jesus
Food/Customs	Fast/meeting place	Variety, hospitable	Word of God

Concerns	Career perfect	Reputations	Others around me
Age	Emphasis power	Senior and elder	generations
Time	Value/respected and dominate	Neglected/ Event oriented	Everything has own time
Observation	Proud people/ superficial	Overall/Plural	Church community
Communication	Direct/demand what they want	indirect	Important/truth
Friendship	Casual	Necessary	God's goal

Another key is to speak in clear terms without using language that assumes previous knowledge. Some people seem unable to communicate the gospel without using theological "church talk." Such terms as *born again*, *atonement*, *saved*, and *sanctification* are foreign to the Muslim.

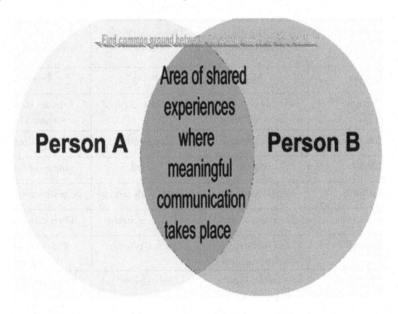

We should also understand stereotypes and misconceptions that Shi'a Muslims and Christians have toward each other. Dismantling these (often false) perceptions will help you in approaching your Shi'a friend. Further, the more your friendship grows, the more your friend will see that perhaps not all his or her beliefs about your culture were true either.

Common Stereotypes

Stereotypes Shi'a Muslims have of Christians	Stereotypes Christians have of Shi'a Muslims	Stereotypes Shi'a Muslims have of Themselves	Stereotypes Shi'a Muslims Consider
All Christians strongly support Israel	All Muslims are the same	Islam is the only way to heaven/universal	Children must be educated in Islamic schools
Materialism	All are "camel jocks" and live in a desert	Have all the answers	We are misunderstood
No moral standard	All Muslims are ignorant	Perfect and moral champion	Family is priority
Independence/ Christians are misinformed	No freedom	Proud of their religion and ancestors	Muslims must maintain a separate Islamic subculture
Individuality	Fanatics/ Terrorists/"religion of sword"	Growing world power and soon will dominate the world	God is on our side

Many Christians use the story of Paul in Athens (Acts 17) as an example for finding cultural and spiritual common ground to connect Shi'a Muslims to Christ. Paul arrived in Athens to share the gospel to the philosophers and the idol-worshippers. Accad writes:

> First we notice that when Paul was in Thessalonica on his way to Athens, he met with fellow Jews on their own turf, the synagogue (Acts 17:1–2, NIV). Second, he didn't say, "come worship with us on Sunday" (the Christian day of worship), but instead went to their place of worship on their holy day … the application for us? How can we expect to win Muslims from the outside? Too often we come across as the all-knowing Westerners, insisting on displacing the cultural and religious customs of people in the Middle East with our own cultural and cultural and religious traditions. We unwittingly say to them, "You are Muslims. We are Western Christians. You have to come to us and follow our ways. If you do not adapt to

our culture and customs, you cannot become members of
God's people." (Accad, 1997)

We should acknowledge the perspective of the Shi'a Muslims. We
have covered some of the cultural differences in another book, but allow
me to share a few more here for purposes of discussion: For many Shi'a
Muslims, clothing is important as a means of preserving a strict moral
ethic. Some may cover their arms and legs. Others may cover their heads
in public as well.

The Shi'a Muslim's view of pets is different from western Christian
views. For example, for many, a dog is seen as an unclean farm animal,
which is something a Shi'a Muslim would never have in his or her
home. When you are inviting a Shi'a Muslim friend to your home,
do not be offended if they avoid your dog or treat it in an unfriendly
manner. If you have a dog in your home, perhaps lock it in a separate
room for the duration of the visit so it is not distracting. Many Shi'a
do not like to touch or be in the presence of household animals,
especially dogs. These are little things to westerns, but they are big to
the Muslim world. Let us do everything in our power to understand
and to make our Shi'a friends feel welcome and comfortable in our
Christian communities and homes.

Some practicing Shi'a Muslims will not eat food that is not prepared
according to Islamic law. Because Muslims have some food restrictions, it
makes it hard for them to choose what to eat if they are at a restaurant or
at Christians' homes. It can be challenging to find "halal meat" prepared
in the proper way. But remember, Shi'a Muslims sometimes have different
ideas about what is clean and acceptable behavior.

Don't put your Bible on the floor or use it for a notebook. To
a Muslim, this is your God's book that gives life and needs to be
respected, regardless of whether they agree with it. With respect to
relationships, do not move too fast, and do not get involved physically
or emotionally with the opposite sex. Be aware that touching may
not be appropriate and may be misinterpreted by your Shi'a Muslim
friend, especially by females. To cross this boundary may be viewed
as insulting in a Muslim family. American Islam tends to be less

restrictive, but Christians should observe conversation protocols until they discern that it is safe to do otherwise.

These are a few examples of cultural differences, but remember, all Shi'a are different. Many that are in the United States are very secular. They have dogs, they drink alcohol, they wear promiscuous clothing, and they do not concern themselves with eating halal food. Some women will cover their heads for photographs just in case it's posted on social media and somebody from home might see it and not approve, but then quickly remove these coverings afterward. This may seem hypocritical—and perhaps on some level it is—but moving to a new land, with a new and very different culture that many have only read about, can be very confusing and overwhelming. Support your Shi'a friends as they navigate this challenging time in their lives. Don't judge, but instead ask questions, and love and support them. They may find this to be very different and refreshing compared to what they might have experienced in their home countries or within their family units if they don't "comply" with Islamic expectations.

7) Share your spiritual story (testimony).

Not every Christian is called to be an evangelist, but all are empowered and commanded to be witnesses (Acts 1:8, NIV). I am still amazed at how God has worked in my life, and I would like others to know about it. The blind man in John 9 is given as an example of this point. As a Christian goes about his or her daily life, he or she should bear witness to Jesus at every opportunity. Every Christian must be prepared to provide an answer to anyone who asks him or her to give the reason for the hope that he or she has. "But in your hearts revere Christ as Lord. Always be prepared to give an answer to everyone who asks you to give the reason for the hope that you have. But do this with gentleness and respect" (1 Peter 3:15, NIV). Shi'a Muslims hear many Christians talking about Jesus Christ, the one they should know about. They don't always know if the story is true, but it usually makes them think.

How would you tell a Shi'a Muslim about Jesus if he or she knew nothing about him? You don't have to know every verse in the Bible or be able to recall it by heart. Simply share your story for his glory. If there is one thing we all have in common as believers, it is the testimony of our lives before and after Christ. Be ready to share your encounters with the living God. When did you first give your life to Jesus? When did you experience the touch of the Holy Spirit? When did you repent and pray to God to save you from your sins in Jesus's name? Your story's main theme is your relationship with your Father in heaven. Speak of your personal background or experience in order to illustrate a point that you are trying to make. Intentionally share your mistakes and struggles, as they might assist your friends in considering solutions that could help. Shi'a seem interested in hearing Christian stories about things that happened in their lives. They enjoy hearing about your Christian experiences and not just your Christian religion. Learn how to share in an effective way, being genuine, joyful, and intentional. Don't focus on past adventures being in the world; but instead, lift Jesus high and glorify him for what he has done to you. One preacher said, "When the sun rises, all stars disappear." Christ is the "Sun of righteousness."

Muslims need me to tell them of true experiences and testimonies, not made-up stories of people who have found hope in the midst of despair. By sharing your story with a Muslim, you are telling him or her, "I want you to meet my Lord Jesus like I did." It was the same when Andrew led his brother Peter to Jesus. "Andrew, Simon Peter's brother was one of the two who heard what John (the Baptist) had said and who had followed Jesus. The first thing Andrew did was to find his brother Simon and tell him, 'We have found the Messiah' (that is the Christ). And he brought him to Jesus" (John 1:40–42, NIV). When Nicodemus came to meet Jesus at night, Jesus told him, "Truly, truly I speak to you, we speak that we do know, and testify that we have seen; and you receive not our witness" (John 13:11, NIV).

So, as a Christian, we must tell Shi'a Muslims what we know about Jesus; what we saw and heard; and about how Jesus touched us (1 John 1:1–4, NIV). Paul shared his testimony three times in Acts: The first time in Acts 9, with the disciples; the second time in Acts 22, with the Jews (his people); and the third time in Acts 26, with the kings and gentiles. By sharing a testimony with a Shi'a, hopefully they might be confronted with the person of Jesus rather than with me as a person or with Christianity as a religion.

We hear of thousands of Shi'a Muslims in the world having encountered

Christ's love and truth through his living word and through dreams and visions and of countless others through seeds planted by obedient believers that others have watered over time. These stories and experience soften the hearts of Shi'a Muslims so that they may want to know more. And as they learn, they will taste and see that the Lord is good (Psalm 34:8, NIV).

Chapter 6: Sharing the Gospel, One on One

Questions for Reflection

1. Think about your church home. Is it welcoming and inviting to *all* who come through the doors? If not, what are some things you can do personally to impact change?

2. When your church host activities, is it always limited to the immediate church community? Are you ever encouraged to invite nonbelievers or people of different cultures? If not, what are some things you can do personally to impact change?

3. Think about the different methods of evangelism. Which resonates most with you and why?

4. Have you ever invited a person or a family from another culture into your home for tea or a meal? If so, please share this experience. If not, can you think of anyone who you could potentially invite?

5. What are your spiritual gifts? How do you think your gifts could be used in evangelism alongside your church community where the body of Christ can work together in different ways?

·· ✖ ··

CHAPTER 7

SHARING THE GOSPEL THROUGH THE CHURCH OR A MINISTRY

I would like to start this section with a biblical statement: "An evangelist is often looked at as a leader within Christian communities." Shi'a Muslim immigrants are often in transition. Their children and their grandchildren are melting into western culture and society. Churches will ultimately need to change as those who remained tied to a specific culture will eventually die out as our country becomes more and more diverse. If the church wants to survive, it must evangelize and open its doors to outsiders, including Shi'a Muslims. To evangelize to the world today, we can begin by reaching out to the foreigners in our own communities. Many of the top leaders in the Muslim world have received training in other countries. Churches can reach Muslim students in the universities near them.

Most Shi'a Muslims who never had a chance to hear about Jesus Christ, find themselves living in Christian communities and in proximity to evangelical churches that share the good news. I am convinced that if Shi'a Muslims interface with the body of Christ, they will be given an opportunity to interface with Christ, be blessed, and be touched by the peace that Christ has given his church.

The following are examples of evangelism that I have found to be effective to Shi'a Muslims. All can be found in scripture. But as with the one-on-one approaches shared in the previous chapter, these are potential starting points intended to inspire and are not all-encompassing. As always, continue to ask the Lord for guidance in each situation and with each person you encounter.

Seven Ways to Evangelize to Shi'a Muslims through a Church or Ministry

1) Invite your Shi'a Muslim friend to church.

Some Christians who evangelize to Muslims regularly might not agree with bringing a Muslim to church. They fear ignorance, aggression, and division in a church environment. Although I agree with them that it can be difficult, I don't see this as an absolute barrier.

How do churches organize themselves in modern societies, and how do these ways of organization shape the churches? Modern Christians describe their churches as communities, yet despite their efforts to build "koinonia," little true community life is to be seen.

Unfortunately, the church today is not the same church mentioned in the gospels. First, the church became a club instead of a community, and Christian members turn to other clubs to meet their economic, political, social, and family needs. Second, the church became an institution. This institution is formally organized with its own internal social systems and its own subculture. Relationships are based on formal contracts and people who join, expecting to offer some services in exchange for some rewards. If they feel they are not receiving what they are worth to the organization, they are free to leave. Third, the church became a place to entertain or perform. Large churches essentially can become crowds.

Shi'a Muslims hesitate to go to church because of the negative assumptions that they have about the church as a whole. They also might notice that many Christians are not enthusiastic, passionate, or lovers of their own church. Some might be judgmental and hypocritical toward others. Your Shi'a friend may raise a lot of questions about your Christian background and your church. What will you tell them? The best answer is to let them discover who Christians are, with all our differences and weaknesses, on their own.

Honestly, it's not so different for any nonbeliever. Many people, regardless of where they are from, have some ideas and stereotypes about the church. Some are based on their own past experiences, or perhaps based on just one or two Christians they know who gave them either a good or bad perception. Some others form opinions based on what they read on social media or what they hear in the media. I know a girl from the same city I live in now who struggled with what she viewed as hypocrisy of Christians. She felt they claimed to believe one thing but did another thing altogether. It was a barrier for her in ultimately accepting the Lord. A wise friend who had witnessed to her finally gave her a very simple truth that opened her eyes and heart: "Just because some of us ruined it, doesn't mean the gospel isn't true."

Most Muslims in western countries (in Europe and in the US) are educated, open-minded, and secular. Thus, they have no problem visiting a Christian church. Our role is to prepare them for what they are going to see and experience with respect to worship, preaching, offerings, prayers, and the way people might act or dress. They should understand the purpose of the church. Shi'as generally enjoy meeting good people through churches, as this parallels their thinking about community. When they come to your church, they may act appropriately and seem to really be enjoying themselves and, to some degree, they might actually be. But often, what is going on inside is quite different. They will compare what they experience in mosques with Christianity and the church. Some have also had other Christian church experiences; some positive and some negative. They may very well be measuring your church against a previous experience.

Although Shi'a Muslims would benefit from you sharing some background with them prior to create some expectations, it's equally helpful for your church community to be prepared. Christians should strive to provide a warm, natural environment and welcoming atmosphere for anyone who walks through the doors. This may seem obvious, but more often than we might like to admit, people who are not regular attendees feel isolated and ignored as we are caught up in our own social circles. Christians need to be honest, sensitive, and transparent. They should not generalize and make any assumptions about Muslims. Like Christians, Muslims can be very different from each other.

Christians should facilitate building friendships and extending themselves and helping to meet everyone's inner need for relationship. Although the church should assimilate and accept newcomers into the fellowship circle, each member of the church has a responsibility to minister when he sees an opportunity and has the authority to do so. Make opportunities available for members to exercise their spiritual gifts in love. If it is your goal to introduce Shi'a Muslims to the spiritual life of Christians, the church is a natural and nonthreatening place to do this.

The objective of going to church is to seek to build our relationships with God and others. The church is a time to make new friends and to reconnect with old ones, to learn about the Bible, and to share our troubles and issues, as well as to thank God for another week of life. But in the church, we also come into the presence of Jesus's bride and of the Holy Spirit. Your Shi'a friend will hear the Spirit and bride say, Come! And let him who hears say, come! Whoever is thirsty, let him come; and whoever wishes, let him take the free gift of the water of life (Revelation 22:17, NIV). Paul's greetings to the church are "Grace and peace to you from God our Father and the Lord Jesus Christ." Shi'a Muslims are seeking the blessing of truth and the Good News. Are we willing to give what we have received?

2) Invite a Shi'a Muslim friend to your home.
I believe a Christian's home should be an extension of the church community. Invite your Shi'a friends to your home with your family or your church small group. In that relaxed environment, it may be easier to ease into conversation about their religion and culture in a nonthreatening way. You may have opportunities to share your faith and culture through that dialogue as well. I know how difficult it is for a Muslim to rid himself of prejudice and open his mind to an objective examination of the Christian faith. Your friend can experience Christ's love in a family setting. As Christians, we believe that relationships are automatically deepened when a person is welcomed into a home. A home can be a place of love and acceptance for many Muslims who are lonely or new to your community. Some might be university students who are far from home for the first time and are especially lonely. Early church gatherings were held in homes of the community, but by the third century, churches had become more like corporations, modeled after Constantine and the Roman government. Today, in postmodern societies, Christians must rediscover the church through homes and family again. Only then will it become a center of true worship, fellowship and mission.

Another opportunity for a church family to involve a Shi'a Muslim and make him or her feel accepted and welcome is by letting the person bring food or cook a meal from his or her own country. Shi'a Muslim people, in general, do not function as individuals. They are closely bonded as families. Therefore, a Christian's home provides an opportunity to have a part in this outreach of love. Because many of them have never set foot inside a Christian home, hosting them during the Christian holidays like Thanksgiving, Christmas, New Year, and Easter have special meaning and give Christians advantages to share Christ. They might raise lots of questions about your faith and even get involved in a home bible study. This is biblical study in action, (Luke 14:12–14; Romans 12:13, NIV). Gathering in homes helps to remove the veil of hate and misinformation that Shi'a may have brought from their countries, or that some in your own home may hold.

It works both ways. A friend of mine does missions work in the Middle East. The group he works with routinely invites Christians from all nations to join them. Part of the experience is to go to a Muslim home for lunch or dinner. One wonderful Muslim family is always happy to host such gatherings. Neither group hides their beliefs, but instead, they choose to focus on what they have in common through which lifelong friendships were formed.

In the homes, the Muslim females of the family often prepare for hours and hours to feed their guests and show them the superior hospitality they are known for in their countries. For many western Christians who visit, their knowledge of Muslims is quite limited to what they see on the news, so the prospect of dining in a Muslim home is often daunting, sometimes even frightening. But over and over, western Christians see walls come down over lively discussions, delicious regional dishes, and smiles. By the time the tea is being poured, everyone is talking like old friends. You may find yourself saying, "Never in my life did I think I would be sitting in a Muslim home, having lunch and being treated so graciously. I had always been taught that Muslims hated us. Yet, all I saw today was love." This is how it happens. An open door can change a lifetime of hate, mistrust, and barriers. Open your doors and see what the Lord will do.

3) Family outreach in the twenty-first century.

Some Christians believe it's helpful to share the gospel with an entire Muslim family. As a family, plan to visit your Shi'a friend's family during the holidays, if they agree, or perhaps even during a time of celebration or distress. Or invite the entire family to your home to share a meal.

Evangelizing to whole families is the pattern of current missionary outreach in parts of the Middle East, North Africa and Asian communities where there is such a strong emphasis on family life. The strategy of sharing the gospel to a whole family is also proving effective in North African villages and tribes, as well as in Kurdistan and Asian communities. The one-on-one approach of individual evangelism doesn't always work as well in such societies. The soundest way for a man to come to Christ is in the setting of his own family.

4) Equipping the church to evangelize.

One of the marks of a healthy church that scholars and preachers talk about frequently in schools and churches is that they have a biblical understanding of evangelism. To evangelize to Shi'a Muslims, Christians need to acknowledge the generation gap among immigrants and adjust their approaches accordingly. When past generations of Shi'a Muslims immigrated to the United States, they wanted to keep their native tongues, cultures, and styles. For them, it was a way to keep part of home with them while they were in a foreign land. It felt safe and comfortable. They chose to open up to and build relationships largely with Christians who were willing to accept their cultures and learn their languages. They are different from the second and third generations. The second generation is still struggling with the issues of language and culture identity. At home, their parents maintain and keep the old ways, but they don't always agree with or understand them. Therefore, the church must find ways to reach out and be sensitive to the unique needs of different generations of Shi'a Muslims in our communities.

I believe the church should have a strategy for evangelism, and the best strategy focus to follow is a biblical one that Jesus gave to his disciples in Acts 1:8, NIV: "But you will receive power when the Holy Spirit comes on you; and you will be my witnesses in Jerusalem, and in all Judea and Samaria, and to the ends of the earth." According to this verse, there are four areas for evangelism—first in Jerusalem, second in Judea, third in Samaria, and fourth in the world. In each of these areas, evangelism might look different. I am going to apply this verse to finding and reaching different generations and types of immigrants.

First, Acts 1:8 speaks of Jerusalem. The Bible says start first spreading the good news in Jerusalem. Where is Jerusalem to you or to your church? Geographically, this is your own community—the Shi'a Muslims who live in your neighborhood, who immigrated a long time ago and who are rooted and melted into the culture and society. We call them the "old generation." They are more open to Christian teachings and are generally not practicing Islam.

Second, Acts 1:8 speaks of the area of Judea. Where is Judea to you and your local church? Geographically, these are the Shi'a Muslims who live in your city but never visited your home or church. They immigrated to America with their parents and straddle two worlds. They often speak two languages fluently, their mother tongues of Arabic or Farsi, and English. We call them the "second and third generations." They may hesitate to come to your church, but they have many questions about Christianity and Christ. They are open to learn about faiths outside of Islam.

Third, Acts 1:8 speaks about the territory of Samaria. The Bible says that after Jerusalem and Judea, we should start spreading the good news in Samaria. Where is Samaria to you and your local church? Geographically, the area expands to Shi'a Muslims who live outside of your community or state but who still reside within America. Culturally, they have refused to assimilate into American culture and society. Religiously, they are not open to Christianity; they do not visit churches and are faithful in Islam.

Fourth, Acts 1:8 speaks of the world. The Bible says after Jerusalem, Judea, and Samaria, go to the world with the good news. Where is the world to you and to your church? Geographically, our focus area expands to Islamic countries and into a global ministry. Culturally, we evangelize in a completely different setting and culture. These Muslims are proud of their culture and often of their religion. They can be aggressive, but at times, they can be open to hearing about other faiths depending upon their needs.

5) Three essential models of evangelism for the church.

People are most open to religious changes after they have immigrated and moved to a new environment. Many Shi'a Muslims coming to your neighborhood have lost their old ties to religious communities and are willing to change. To evangelize to them, we should live alongside them and build relationships and trust. Effective evangelism is God's will for the church (2 Corinthians 5:19–20, NIV). When the church loses its evangelistic motivations, the sentence is spiritual death. No amount of study, love, sharing, or serving will save the church when there is no element of evangelism. This should always be a priority for the church and for Christians. Although we can use a wide variety of evangelistic models, our job as Christians is to be creative, understand, and teach the evangelistic models that are most suitable and effective for our church. I'd like to provide several models as a starting point. These are models that can be taught to a church or ministry community as whole. Different models will appeal to different people within those groups based upon their individual personalities and spiritual gifts.

The first essential evangelistic model is the natural way. Many Christians in the church like to use this model. They enjoy evangelizing through the way they live and lead their lives as Christians in the church. Anyone who think of him- or herself as a "people person" will especially thrive with this model. Many of these people prefer discussing a Shi'a person's life before getting into the details of their beliefs and opinions. They enjoy long talks with Shi'a friends, and it doesn't matter much where the conversation goes. People generally consider them to be interactive, sensitive, and caring people. If the Shi'a sees their love for others, they might ask questions about their faith and seek answers. As a Shi'a watches their lives and compare them with others in the world, they might ask, "What makes this person different?" As such, a critical element of evangelism to them is going to be observing unity among church members. Since Shi'a Muslims emphasize community, it is important that the Christian group also demonstrate a strong community when witnessing to them. Jesus prayed for his disciples to be united in the world. Shi'a Muslims are a community-oriented race crying out for relationships with others who need love and a sense of belonging. If we consider the life of Jesus himself, we will see that he lived a life of community with his Father and his disciples.

Humbly acting in perfect obedience to the Father's will meant that Jesus also lived in fellowship with others. Therefore, a church community should maintain effective communication and develop a structure that will incorporate opportunities for building a natural evangelism with Shi'a Muslims.

Natural evangelistic models use church programs to witness to Shi'a friends. This kind of evangelism not only reaches Americans, but also the Shi'as. For example, start a children's bible club in Christian homes and invite Shi'a children to attend. This kind of evangelism could open doors to evangelize to the whole Shi'a Muslim's family (parents, sisters, brothers, and relatives). Researchers have found that in the United States, more than 85 percent of those who receive Christ do so before they reach the age of fourteen. Invite children of your Muslim neighbors to a weekly Bible club meeting in your home or backyard. Also, vacation bible schools are effective in reaching Muslim kids during the summers or holidays. Activities could include sports, arts and crafts, field trips, bible stories, memory verses, songs, and refreshments.

Shi'a Muslims have a great network and support group of women, but in Christianity, we rarely provide that in our churches. I believe that Christian women will play a major role in the lives of Shi'a women. As a Christian woman, you can enter the kitchen and cook and have a cup of tea with a Shi'a Muslim peer. A Christian woman can sometimes enter into deep conversation with other women more easily. I've ever heard of some Shi'a Muslim women relating more closely to Christian women than to her husband. Once her husband knows that you are not like other Christian women in American society and you are taking care of his wife, the door will be open for the whole home to trust and listen to you.

Planned debates should be entered into only after much prayer and by the guidance of the Holy Spirit. Choose a topic related to Christianity and Islam and invite your church to a hall or a room to hear several knowledgeable persons debate each side of the argument. We found many debates in the New Testament like with Stephen and the Jews in Jerusalem (Acts 6:9–10, NIV); Paul, with the philosophers in the marketplace at Athens (Acts 17:18, NIV); and in the synagogues and lecture halls of Tyrranus in Ephesus (Acts 19:8–10, NIV). After each speaker gives a presentation or small lecture, there is an opportunity for others to respond. Consider some potential pitfalls.

Usually, Muslims will often rally a large group from their communities to the debate, greatly outnumbering the Christians. Usually when people leave a Christian-Muslim debate, both sides think that their side has won. Often, the debates are videotaped, edited in the Muslim's favor, and distributed in the Muslim communities to motivate Islam da'wah (call).

Church counseling also offers opportunities to show Muslims care and love in helping them with their problems from a Christian perspective. Many Muslims come to my office seeking help in counseling, even those I have never met before. Most of them respect and trust Christian ministers. They ask me for help and for advice; they even accept me as their counselor about their marriage problems, health, economic problems, immigration questions, employment, sexual problems, family problems, and more. This is an opportunity to share your concern for them as a Christian and to show Christ's love and care. It is also a great opportunity to share Christ's salvation, to pray, and to open a way for the Holy Spirit to touch their lives and heal them.

The second essential evangelistic model is the direct way. If I had to choose the model that is most aligned with my personality, this would be it. In conversations, I like to approach topics directly without "beating around the bush." I do not have a problem confronting my Shi'a friends with the truth even if I risk damaging the friendship. I am not shy to identify myself with a church even if my Shi'a friend doesn't like my church. I challenge him or her as is necessary. I am not sensitive about everything and just speak the truth plainly! I sometimes get in trouble for lacking a certain gentleness and sensitivity in the way I interact with the Shi'a. A motto that would fit me perfectly is, "Make a difference or a mess, but do *something* for Christ." It is a little aggressive, and usually few Christians in the United States support or are comfortable with this style of evangelism. It requires courage, love, and wisdom. But I see many Shi'a Muslims repent and receive Christ as their savior and Lord through this evangelistic direct model.

People within the church can use this model by finding out where Muslims live, what activities they do, and what type of Shi'a Muslims they are, and then going out to find them. Or set and organize outreach meetings in your church, often called "revival meetings," and invite them in. Send an invitation to your Shi'a friends for special events during the holidays or invite them to a special occasion and deliver a clear message about Christ with an altar call. You can also invite a worship band or a famous singer to these events. The church can set a booth at the Arab or Persian festivals in your city if you have those. The church can come together to do door-to-door evangelism, distribute tracts, and put a piece of Christian literature or a Jesus movie into their hands.

The church can use the media to confront Shi'a Muslims with the message of the gospel. The media is playing a major role in your Shi'a Muslim's life. In small communities, basic information is communicated by word of mouth. In cities, Muslim people depend on the media and social media for general knowledge. To inform the city about Christ, the church must make effective use of social media and the satellite media available to it.

Christian satellite and social media have an incredible impact on the Shi'a Muslim world. For the first time ever, we notice that many Christians and Shi'a Muslims have satellite TVs. Many Christian satellite programs criticize Islam openly. Presently, they are presenting more psychological-oriented topics, discussions, programs, and interviews to help Shi'a Muslims gain awareness of the mental and emotional aspects, needs, and struggles facing all human beings while also leading them to Christ. Some of these programs go so far as to discredit the Qur'an. Many young Shi'a Muslims are reacting and questioning the Qur'an because of these programs. Many Christians who are preaching and teaching the word of God via satellite TV are challenging Shi'a Muslims and their beliefs. For example, Ravi Zachariah is confronting Muslims to rethink their religion and challenging them with difficult questions that even their leaders cannot answer. Muslim scholars complain of the huge numbers of Muslims turning their lives over to Christ. Ravi Zachariah has said, "I want my message to be shocking, shaking, and sharp to Muslims."

Similarly, friendly and direct discussions of the gospel with a Shi'a Muslim through internet chat rooms may help to win him or her to Christ. Through the internet and through email, one can speak without exposing him- or herself to acts of violence and can share with courage and boldness.

Partnership is essential in sharing the gospel in a direct way. We do not plan or attempt to reach out alone in our church. We find it is best to work in teams. There is an increase in power and blessings when two or three are gathered in Jesus's name to do his work. I will give a few biblical examples on how to guide Shi'a Muslims into the gospel and to win them to Christ. In John 12:20, NIV, Greeks came to Jerusalem searching for the Messiah. On their way, they met Christians. "Now there were some Greeks among those who went up to worship at the feast. They came to Philip, who was from Bethsaida in Galilee, with a request. Sir, they said, 'we would like to see Jesus.' Philip went to tell Andrew; Andrew and Philip in turn told Jesus." The beauty in this story is that Philip and Andrew depended on each other in guiding the Greeks to meet Jesus in person and did not enter into a competition over the strangers, but together worked hand in hand for one purpose, the salvation of the Greeks. In 1 Corinthians 3:5–6, NIV, Paul writes, "I planted the seed, Apollos watered it, but God made it grow." Christians need to learn how to work together for the sake of the gospel. Partnership requires openness to weaknesses and strengths, sharing concerns, agreeing, and listening. Another example is Paul's mission: Paul, Silas, and Lydia demonstrated a leadership model where mutual understanding and dialogue facilitated partnership that resulted in a Christian community in Philippi (Acts 16:11–40, NIV). We also see in Acts 18:1–4 and in 18:24–26 that Paul, Priscilla, Aquila, and Apollo as missionary partners and tent makers.

While evangelizing, communication and friendship are important to create strong partnerships among Christian workers. Empowering and praying for one another is also important. Establish a prayer community of faithful partners who will commit to praying for your and those you are reaching out to. In the end, share resources and establish a network among churches that can help increase your outreach efforts.

The third essential evangelistic model is the indirect way. Many Christians call it "friendship evangelism." They rarely mention that they are Christians at all. I call them "nice-Christians," like Dorcas in Acts 9:36–42. This woman lived in Joppa and was known for always doing good and helping the poor.

Christians who believe in this model prefer a long relationship and genuine friendship. They see needs in people's lives that others often overlook. They find fulfillment in helping others, often in behind-the-scenes ways. They would rather show love through actions than through words. They have found that quiet demonstrations of love and care sometimes help people open up and become more receptive to what they think. They are more practical and action-oriented than they are philosophical and idea-oriented. They pursue ways to help Shi'a Muslims who have practical needs that must be met through social work, language, medical services, food, and everyday problem-solving. They offer assistance that is cultural, personal, and spiritual. Christians offer Shi'a a wide variety of programs. These range from recreational activities to the more spiritually based meetings that raise questions about Christianity and its origins. Organize events through your church, such as picnics, trips, camping, pizza parties, talent shows, and sports. The church cannot only help newcomers find a place to live, clothing, and food, but they can also help them acclimate to life in their new land.

Christians can encourage the church to donate and collect household items and furniture to distribute to Shi'a Muslims in need. This shows hospitality, and hospitality is a way of life for the Middle Easterner, and thus, it plays a very important role in church evangelism. The church should have a program designed to help with ESL (English as a second language) needs. Without a doubt, one of the hardest things to endure in a foreign country is the inability to communicate effectively. The need to communicate and meet educational goals also provides us with an opportunity to work with the Shi'a. Christians can recruit English-speaking people who are gifted in languages to help your Shi'a Muslim friends. If your Shi'a Muslim friend shows interest in the Bible, you can teach him or her English through the Bible. When teaching the Bible, always remember that most Shi'a Muslims don't understand the language of the Bible, so it is important to use terms that are clear or stop to explain a word or phrase.

The Bible is clear that the followers of Christ belong to a new people that take priority over their old worldly identities. If Christians do not learn to live and express their unity, the church will become a part of the world's structures that perpetuate poverty, divisions, hostilities, and wars.

Ways of Evangelim

All approaches are essential for evangelism to the Arab Muslims
All ways must be integrated, since each has limitations

Indirect Evangelism/ Life Witness					Direct Evangelism/ Verbal
Education English Partners Transportation Help moving Give away items Outing Sport events Shopping	Hosting Holidays Thanksgiving Christmas Easter	Hospitality Visitations	Medical Help, Relief		Outreach Festivals Bible and trucks Distribution Revival meetings & worship Open air evangelism Obvious Booths Media Debates

Things to Consider:

Perhaps you've wanted to share your faith but are not sure how you'd convince a Shi'a Muslim to believe in the truth of Christ. If this has crossed your mind, stop right there! It's not your job to convince anyone of anything. Think about it. Hebrews 11:1 says, "Now faith is confidence in what we hope for and assurance about what we do not see." Think about it. We do not live in the days when Jesus walked among us; rather, our faith is in *what we do not see.* Now, using the Bible along with countless historical texts and archeological facts, we can make very compelling arguments in support of Jesus's life, death, and resurrection as well as many biblical events. Further, we can look at the fulfillment of many biblical prophecies to make our case for the legitimacy of Christianity. But ultimately, the very definition of "faith" makes it virtually impossible to definitively prove.

Have you ever tried to prepare for an exam when you weren't certain what material would be covered and then studied all night only to find that you focused on all the wrong things? It's the same principle. When sharing the gospel, we are dealing with the human element. We do not know what will resonate with people. We do not know what they might ask. We do not know their histories or experiences. We do not know what seeds have been planted by God to prepare their hearts. So, instead of spending countless hours creating an airtight case before you venture out, focus on continuing to grow in your knowledge of the word and of God's character. But know that you will continue learning and growing in the Lord until you take your last breath, never having "arrived." Spend some time learning about Islam to know at least in concept where your friends are coming from. But know that you will likely never be an expert. Ask for wisdom. Pray often. Listen to the Holy Spirit.

Sure, some people are drawn to facts, but so many former Shi'a Muslims I speak with tell me that, although they had questions along the way, it was not hard facts that "convinced" them of the truth. It was truly a supernatural experience; for some, just one moment. For others, it was a series of small moments over the course of several years. But for all, God had touched their hearts in a wonderfully unique way, and they were forever changed.

Think about your own experience in coming to the Lord. Did anyone truly "convince" you with a book or series of facts? Or did God, in his infinite mercy and grace, touch your heart in such a way that you "just knew"? We all have unique experiences and backgrounds (and the associated baggage that comes with that), but ultimately, no matter where we are from, what we've been through, or what languages we speak, as humans, we share common ground. We all desire relationship—genuine encounters with each other—and the truth. So I encourage you to step out in faith and love and let God do the "convincing" in the hearts of those in front of you.

PART FOUR

Reaching Shia Muslims for Christ is the first step, but then what? It is critical to bring them into fellowship and community with other believers and to be intentional about discipleship to create a solid foundation of faith. Chapter seven, eight, nine and ten are sample discovery course for effective discipleship, input from the field and evaluation to help with follow up the new believers and create intentional discipleship in your community church.

Many churches have discipleship programs, but when discipling Muslim converts to Christ, there are important nuances. And, many courses presuppose a fair amount of Christian understanding from our Western Judeo-Christian culture. Certain basic principles such as God's goodness are taken for granted.

This sample discovery course has been used to teach Muslim converts to Christ foundation truths of the faith. It covers practical matters such as group size, location, effective leadership and handling conflict as well as sample curriculum complete with objective, biblical verse readings and follow up questions to prompt thought and reflection.

Proper preparation can help the Shi'a student to reap a rich harvest. God, who created the universe, who controls history, and who will accomplish His plan in His perfect timing has chosen to speak through His Word. This study exposes a person to the Word of God. God's word is powerful, changes the heart of people, and creates life and understanding. God's Word doesn't change. God's revelation did not come in the English language or through the western culture. The student, who is familiar with the ancient Near Eastern culture, is able to understand some passages in the Bible better than someone from another part of the world because he or she would be familiar with that culture and that region. The teacher has to allow the Bible to speak for itself. The more we encourage people to read the Word, the more it will speak into their life and touch their hearts.

CHAPTER 8

THE TRUTH ABOUT CHRIST, A NINE-WEEK DISCOVERY STUDY COURSE SAMPLE

Our focus in these chapters has been about evangelizing to Shi'a Muslims. But once they accept Christ as their personal Lord and Savior, what's next?

It's important to involve them in a bible study and in your church community, but, like any new believers, they will need focused discipleship. I'd like to present an outline of a nine-week discovery study course that I personally use when discipling a new convert to Christ. I will provide some elements that I feel are important for creating a solid foundation for the new believer, particularly one who is coming from a very different perspective and knows a very different god than the God of Abraham, Isaac, and Jacob.

I would encourage you to use this framework to develop a curriculum that works for you and the individuals and groups you are serving. Pray, meet in groups with your pastor and church leaders to discuss, and create a course that is uniquely yours.

Objective

The idea behind this course is to present major, foundational concepts about God and Christ to the Shi'a Muslims: either one who has received Christ, or one who is merely willing to take a good look at the Bible. Because it is hard to predict how long a "seeker" will study with you, the course is designed to be short, while still presenting the most important truths of the gospel in nine lessons. Our primary audience for the course is Muslims or Muslim converts to Christianity, but it certainly has other applications with any new believer, regardless of his or her background.

It seems that many discipleship courses presuppose too much Christian understanding. Certain basic principles, such as God's goodness, are taken for granted. As a result, many courses begin in the New Testament. I have felt, however, that we must start at the beginning, in Genesis.

First, this study considers the basic truths of the first five sample lessons taken from Genesis 1–3, by asking: Who is God? What is God's purpose for his creatures, the basic quality of creation? Who are humans? What is humanity's relationship to God? Who is Satan? What are Satan's purposes and his strategies? What is the fall of humanity? What is sin, and what are its consequences? While investigating these questions, we will explore the problem of humanity and the universe. The latter subjects can be summed up as our present terrible condition in contrast to his once-perfect condition, an exposure of humankind's sinful nature and the need for God to rescue us and put things right. If the Shi'a seekers or new believers have a good grasp on the Genesis account of these things, then they will have come a long way toward the gospels making sense. Many scholars and theologians agree that, in discipling those from non-Christian cultures, one must begin with Genesis.

The last four sample lessons concentrate on the core themes of blood sacrifices, substitutions, and atonement in the Old Testament, in Genesis 3:15, 3:21–24, Genesis 4, and the promises and the account of Cain and Abel. The eighth lesson is about God's response to faith, studying Abraham's willingness to offer his son, Isaac, to God in Genesis 22, and the common links between the story of Isaac in the Old Testament and Jesus in the New Testament. There is a brief look ahead at Christ as the ultimate atoning sacrifice, but the emphasis is on setting the stage from the Old Testament so that, when we get to Christ, it makes sense. Thus, the nine weeks on these core truths are an indispensable start. Our preference is to make the lessons as expository as possible. Along those lines, we have found it best for groups to learn through discussion. Some of the material will simply have to be taught, but whenever possible, it is best for the teacher to ask leading questions and to allow the students to discover the truths for themselves. Not only does this keep them from getting bored, but it also helps the truths stick in their minds, and hopefully in their hearts as well.

Sample Summary of Lessons

1. Who is God? The Basic Quality of Creation (Genesis 1)
2. God's Purpose for Humanity and Creature (Genesis 2)
3. Humankind's Relationship with Creation (Genesis 2:18–25)
4. Devil and Temptation (Genesis 3:1–7; Matthew 4:1–11)
5. The Fall: The Origin of Sin and Its Consequences (Genesis 3:8–24)
6. God's Promises for Salvation (Genesis 3:15; 21–24)
7. Solution in the Torah: Cain and Abel's Sacrifices (Genesis 3:15; 4)
8. Solution in the Torah: Abraham Sacrificing Isaac (Genesis 22)
9. Solution in the New Testament: Jesus as a sacrifice (John 1:1–18)

Practical Matters

Group Size, Format, and Preparation

The most effective group size is between one and seven students. A large group might cause some to become silent or even some to gang up together against the biblical material. In many cases, the studies only mention the point to be made. You will need to work out how you want to explain it or whether you think it needs further explanation. The material is not especially contextualized, but it certainly can be used, even without adaptation, in the context of a highly contextualized ministry (e.g., a "Jesus Muslim" approach). Design each study to be forty-five to sixty minutes long. In addition, you may want to have singing, sharing, and prayer; drills for finding verses; or whatever else you see as appropriate for your group and where they are at.

As you anticipate exploring seven lessons, you may feel excited or fearful. The teacher may assign students something to study ahead of time, but this is not necessary and, in some situations, might cause an impediment for some to continue. It may be more fruitful to have the students memorize verses that they've just studied and then to review these memorized verses at the beginning of the following week. If possible, there should be a Bible for each student, using the same translation for all. I suggest using the NIV translation. If you are dealing with illiterate people, there should be time for slow and expressive reading of the text, and key verses should be recited many times.

The design of the sample course is a gradual build-up for six lessons, with the seventh lesson calling for a decision if one has not yet been made. The teacher should stay focused on the passage being discussed and keep the discussion on track. When a question arises that is not related to the passage or the lesson being discussed, postpone discussing it until later. Be willing to share your ideas, observations, and questions with everyone in the group. Keep in mind that some people speak up readily, while others prefer to be quiet and to think quietly. You should treat everyone in the group equally; everyone's views are important.

In preparation, the teacher should plan to spend at least one to two hours with the biblical texts and this material. Be flexible with the start of your lesson, but make sure you end on time. Remember that you're ministering the word of God, not just reading through a guidebook.

Combine people from various countries and put together them in one group. This can be difficult unless you pray, pray, and pray in order to feel God's peace and presence. Everyone is bringing his or her own spiritual beliefs, personal baggage, and ideological thinking to the group. Remember that every human being has common spiritual needs, but each one also has diverse ideas. If we say to people of the nations, "God is love," Shi'a Muslims may have a difficult time understanding what that means because their god is punitive. The Hindu might say, "Which god are you talking about?" A Buddhist might not understand this concept because his god is impersonal. An atheist would say that there is no god.

Proper preparation can help the Shi'a student to reap a rich harvest. God, who created the universe, who controls history, and who will accomplish his plan in his perfect timing, has chosen to speak through his word. This study exposes a person to the word of God. God's word is powerful, changes the heart of people, and creates life and understanding. God's word doesn't change. God's revelation did not come in the English language or through the western culture. The student who is familiar with the ancient Near Eastern culture, is able to understand some passages in the Bible better than someone from another part of the world because he or she would be familiar with that culture and that region. The teacher should allow the Bible to speak for itself. The more we encourage people to read the word, the more it will speak into their lives and touch their hearts.

The teacher must know that Genesis is not a book of science, though scientists are right to investigate its claims. It is not a biography or a history book, but rather, it is a book of theology. God doesn't contradict himself. His purpose from the beginning was to create life. Remember that your purpose is to provide students with exposure to the truth. You are there to help them understand God's purpose for them, how to build a relationship with him, and to see that without the word of God and without Jesus, there is no life or hope for the future.

Many debate the question of which type of teaching is most fruitful in discipleship: biblical content, or a so-called "obedience-oriented" teaching. To us, the question is akin to which wing of an airplane is most important. Clearly, focusing exclusively on one style is detrimental to the other and can short-circuit the new believer's walk with Christ. Many verses could be given to prove the necessity of both. The disciple who is fed only content, truths, and theology week after week is left unchallenged in his or her faith and may be continuing with a variety of unhealthy motivations. Likewise, the disciple who is merely given the commands of Christ to obey as sort of challenges, but who is not helped to grow in the "knowledge of Christ," is likely to suffer from a real lack of depth in the long run, resulting in a lack of the spiritual understanding necessary to make the right choices in life. May God use you greatly as Christ is reproduced in those you are called to disciple!

First Things First: Examine your Motives
Our role as Christians and as brothers and sisters of new Shi'a believers in Christ is to stand with them. Stop and ask yourself some important questions before you begin. For example, do you understand the cost of their faith choice? Will they have Christian friends to stand by, support, and accept them? Do you understand their cultures and values? Do you know their struggles and needs? Do you have the spiritual maturity needed to teach and disciple others? Do you love and respect them?

Offer Your Support

We need to encourage our Shi'a friends that they will not be alone. Be sure to encourage them to seek spiritual truths by teaching them about the basics of Christianity. New believers need to grow in faith and biblical knowledge if they are planning to move back to their home countries because it's unlikely (if not dangerous) for them to find strong spiritual support and Christian fellowship.

Keep in Touch

If your new friends travel or visits home on an extended trip, keep in touch! Encourage them with God's own words or promises, and affirm them with the assurance that you will keep them daily in your prayers. Write and send letters, emails, and gifts of encouragement and love. Explain to them how important it will be for them to find a group of believers or a church that will be supportive, both spiritually and emotionally. Prior to their departure, do try to understand some of the challenges or issues they may face in their home countries. Be sensitive to these things in correspondence or conversations that may be monitored.

Find an Appropriate Local Small Group That Could Help Them

The best source of fellowship is a small group in the local church, made up of people who identify with each other or who have had similar experiences. They can help a new Shi'a believer on many levels because they themselves have traveled that road. They have experienced struggles with issues like job-hunting, corruption, tensions with their families, community relationships, and marriages. This small group should understand the unique tension and confusion for new believers who come from Shi'a Muslim backgrounds. They should know the persecution that they might face here in United States or in their countries when or if they go back to their families. The group needs to keep the door open for their friends to come back if they are attacked by their families or communities because of their new faith in Jesus. Your Shi'a friends may be in a dangerous situation. When a Shi'a becomes your brother or sister in Christ, you should do what you can to support and protect him or her.

Don't Try to Act Perfect or Be Afraid to Make Mistakes

Be yourself. We often make mistakes with new Shi'a believers. When this happens, learn from your mistakes, move forward, and avoid making the same mistake twice. Don't give up. There are common mistakes that we make in working with converted Shi'a. One mistake is giving him or her too much at once and not narrowing your objectives for each time you meet together. Another is leading him or her on by asking for his or her opinion about your program but never giving him or her a chance to see it or be involved in it. Another mistake is talking down to your new friend instead of treating him or her as an equal or misleading him or her in "small things," such as saying a meeting will last for a one hour, but then keeping it going for much longer. A new Shi'a convert needs trust, understanding, and love.

Yet another mistake is not being sufficiently flexible with your schedule to meet with your Shi'a friend on weekends, evenings, and other times that suit his or her schedule. When working with a converted Shi'a, be sensitive to his or her cultural orientation. Americans tend to rush things. Be slow and intentional in teaching him or her about God.

Addressing Practical Needs

To disciple a Shi'a friend not only means that you are providing spiritual counseling, but also caring for physical and practical needs. Some are ready to change their religions for the sake of money or to gain respect and protection. One of the mistakes many make is not preparing the community to accept them. Another is being overly excited, asking them to give a testimony of their faith from the pulpit in front of a large group before they are ready or feel comfortable.

Common Questions

Be prepared to answer some challenging questions, including, who is the God of Christianity? Does God really exist? Why did God create human beings? Why do the innocent people have to suffer? What is sin? Why did they offer sacrifices in the Old Testament times? What is God's purpose for humanity? Has the Bible been corrupted? Why do Christians worship "three Gods"? Who was Jesus Christ? Who is the Holy Spirit? Is there really a Triune God? Why do Christians insist on the Crucifixion? Why do so many Christians live an unholy lifestyle? Why do you have so many denominations in Christianity? Who is be saved? Do the Qur'an and the Bible agree, and why does this matter? Why do you have four gospels?

The following are sample lessons shared from my own curriculum designed to get you started in a rich discipling program. As previously stated, I believe that a strong biblical foundation that is focused on the basics, will create strong roots for a new convert to Christianity to grow upon.

Sample Discovery Lesson #1

Who Is God?
The purpose of this lesson:
1. To explore basic ideas of who the God of the Bible is and how he created humanity.
2. To put aside former beliefs or ideas about Christianity.
3. To create foundational truths that, if understood correctly, will provide an excellent start. But if misinterpreted, they will potentially cause a new believer to be "off" in his or her basic understanding of God and the purpose of life.

Read: Genesis 1:1–26
Brief Overview of Genesis 1:1–26 (use simple words and terminology)

Sample Questions:
Q1: Try to imagine what God had in mind before he started creating. What comes to mind?

Q2: In the beginning was God, but who created God?

Q3. Describe what you think it was like before God formed the universe.

Q4. List what he created on each day. Why does God first form the world (on days one to three) and then fill that world (on days four to six)?

Q5. How did God create what he did?

Q6. In what ways do you think God views his creation as being good?

Q7. What can you learn about God from his spoken word? What is your impression of him?

Q8. What does the story of creation reveal about the trinity?

Q10. How does the God of the Bible differ from other gods of the world religions in the context of creation?

Q11. How would you respond to one who reads the daily horoscope, believing that the position of the sun, moon, and stars ordain our personalities and state?

Sample Application Questions:
Q1: What gifts has God given to you that enable you to create?

Q2. What are some parallels between the Holy Spirit's work in creation and in your personal life?

Q3. Can you see any similarities between yourself and the God of the Bible?

Memory verse: Genesis 1:1, NIV: "In the beginning God created the heavens and the earth."

Sample Discover Lesson # 2

God's Purpose for Humans and the Creatures of the Earth
The purpose of the lesson:
   1. To introduce and discuss who God is and why he made men and women (our relationship with God).
   2. To expose incorrect teachings about our creator in the light of biblical truths.

Rev. Dr. Elie Hasbani

Read: Genesis 1:26–2:14
Brief Overview of Genesis 1:26–2:14

Sample Questions:
Q1: What is God's image? Is it something physical?

Q2: How do you feel about the idea that you are made in God's image and likeness?

Q3. Are only men made in the image of God? Are women too? Consider that man needs woman in order to be in God's image fully. In what ways are man and woman unique among God's creation?

Q4: How did God distinguish between human beings and other creatures? Are animals made in God's image?

Q5. Why did God decide to rest on the seventh day?

Q6. Why did God create a perfect paradise for humanity?

Q7. Why did God place the tree of knowledge of good and evil in the middle of the beautiful garden and tell Adam and Eve not to eat from it?

Q8. How many kinds of trees were there?

Q10. What were you taught about the Garden of Eden that God had prepared for Adam?

Sample Application Questions:
Q1. What shows God's love for man? List three to four things.

Q2. As you look around at God's creation, how does it give you a greater appreciation for the creator?

Q3. How have these passages helped you understand who you were created to be in relation to God?

Q4. In what areas do you need to trust God in your life?

Memory Verse: Genesis 1:26, NIV: "Then God said: 'Let us make man in our image, in our likeness, and let rule over the fish of the sea and the birds of the air, over the livestock, over all the earth, and over all the creatures that moves along the ground.'"

Sample Discovery Lesson #3

Humanity's Relationship with Creation
The purpose of the lesson:
1. To discover our relationship with each other and the creatures around us.
2. To learn why it is not good for man to be alone.
3. To understand the roles and lives of Adam and Eve as God intended them.

Read: Genesis 2:15–25
Brief Overview of Genesis 2:15–25

Sample Questions:
Q1. If God knows everything ahead of time, why did he give Adam the limitation of not eating from the tree of knowledge?

Q2. How do you define "helper"? Does "helper" sound like a lesser person? An equal person? A greater person?

Q3. How did Adam come up with all the names for the animals?

Q4. What is significant about God creating woman last?

Q5. Why did God create Eve from Adam's ribs if God wanted them to be equal? Why didn't God make them at the same time?

Q6. Explain in your own words what verse 24 teaches us about marriage.

Q7. What does it mean that Adam and Eve were "naked and they felt no shame"?

Sample Application Questions:

Q1: Have you ever felt alone? How has this passage helped you understand who you were created to be in relation to your family, creatures of the earth, and other people?

Q2: What do you need from this group to help feel more connected to others?

Q3: What about God's love and purpose for the family? What did you learn from this passage about your relationships with people of the opposite sex?

Memory Verse: Genesis 2:24: "For this reason a man will leave his father and mother and be united to his wife, and they will become one flesh."

Sample Discovery Lesson #4

The Devil and Temptation

The purpose of this lesson:

1. Part 1 is intended to expose the devil and to understand how we can resist his temptations.
2. Part 2 is intended explain the origin and effects of personal sin.

Read: Genesis 3:1–6

Brief Overview of Genesis 3:1–6

Sample Questions:
Q1: Who was the serpent? What does the serpent represent?

Q2: Where did Satan come from?

Q3: What are the other names of Satan?

Q4. What attracted Eve to sin?

Q5. What statements does the serpent make about the purpose and results of the instructions God gave?

Q6. How have the serpent's words distorted Eve's thinking?

Q7. What was Satan's strategy?

Q8. What is the difference between a temptation and a test?

Sample Application Questions:
Q1. Why do you think Adam eats the fruits if could he have resisted? What should he have done?

Q2. What one lesson have you learned from this study that can help you recognize and resist a temptation you are facing?

Memory Verse: Genesis 3:6, NIV: "When the woman saw that the fruit of the tree was good for food and pleasing to the eye, and also desirable for gaining wisdom, she took some and ate it. She also gave some to her husband, who was with her, and he ate it."

Sample Discovery Lesson #5

Sin and the Fall

The purpose of this lesson:
1. To define sin and its consequences.
2. To address the penalty for breaking the law of God.

Read Genesis 3: 7–24
Brief Overview of Genesis 3:7

Sample Questions:

Q1: After Adam and Eve disobeyed God, why did they then realize that they were naked and hide from God?

Q2: How do you define sin and its consequences?

Q3: Why didn't God destroy the serpent immediately?

Q4: Why didn't God destroy Adam and Eve and then begin all over again with another couple?

Sample Application Question:

Q1: Think of a time you sinned. What were the consequences?

Memory Verse: Genesis 3:15, NIV: "And I will put enmity between you and the woman, and between your offspring and hers; he will crush your head, and you will strike his heel."

Sample Discovery Lesson # 6

God's Promises for Salvation

The purpose of this lesson:
1. To show God's holiness.
2. To reveal God's promises.

Read: Genesis 3:15, 21–24
Brief Overview of Genesis 3:15, 21–14

Sample Questions:
Q1: Who is the "seed of the woman"?

Q2: How did Satan strike the heel of the Messiah?

Q3: How will Christ (the seed of woman) crush Satan's head?

Q4. How did God respond to the devil and sin?

Sample Application Questions:
Q1. If Jesus is the promised tree of life, what does that mean to us as sinners?

Q2. If Jesus is the promised "seed," what does that mean to us?

Q3. Where in this story do you find any good news?

Memory Verse:

Sample Discovery Lessons #7

Solution in the Torah

(Cain and Abel's Sacrifices)
The purpose of this lesson:
1. Solutions and redemption.
2. Continuity of generational sin.

Read: Genesis 4:1–18
Brief Overview of Genesis 4:1–18

Rev. Dr. Elie Hasbani

Sample Questions:
Q1. Do you think Adam and Eve ever told their sons about the fig leaves and the coats of skins?

Q1. What was Cain's occupation?

Q2. What was Abel's occupation?

Q3. What offering did Cain bring?

Q4. What offering did Abel bring?

Q5. Which offering was pleasing to God?

Q6. Why did God accept Abel's, but not Cain's sacrifice?

Q7. What happened after God refused Cain's sacrifice?

Q8. Why did Cain murder Abel?

Q9. Why does anger exist?

Sample Application Questions:
Q1. What is the answer? Good works or faith?

Q2. What do you do to gain control of the bad behaviors in your life?

Sample Memory Verse: Genesis 4:6, 9, NIV: "The Lord said to Cain, 'Why are you angry? Why is your face downcast? If you do what is right, will you not be accepted?' … Then the Lord said to Cain, 'Where is your brother Abel?'"

**Consider asking the class for a decision or recommitment to Christ during this lesson.

Sample Discovery Lesson #8

Solution in the Torah

The purpose of this lesson:
1. To see an example of salvation by faith in the Old Testament.
2. To show God's faithfulness to those who believe in him.
3. To show the covenant was given to Isaac and not to Ishmael.
4. To recognize the new covenant by the Lamb of God that is Jesus in the New Testament.
5. To see the connection between both Old and New Testaments.
6. To see God's fulfillment of His Word and promises.

Read Genesis 22:1–14
Brief Overview of Genesis 22:1–14

Sample Questions:
Q1. Have you ever felt tested by God? How did you respond?

Q2. What is the difference between temptation and testing?

Q3: What is God asking of Abraham?

Q4. Why does Abraham have to offer Isaac, and not Ishmael, his firstborn?

Q5. Why did Abraham have to sacrifice a burnt offering, the innocent ram, on the mountaintop? If he was a righteous man, why then did he have to sacrifice his son?

Q6. How did Abraham respond to God's calling?

Q7. Do you think Abraham actually would have killed Isaac?

Q8. Why did God wait until the last second to stop Abraham?

Q9. What do you think Isaac felt as he walked with his father?

Sample Application Questions:

Q1: Since God already made his covenant with Abraham, why should he test him and then offer the same covenant again?

Q2: Consider some parallels between Isaac in this story and Jesus's crucifixion

Memory Verse: Genesis 22:7-8, NIV: "The fire and wood are here," Isaac said, "but where is the lamb for the burnt offering?" Abraham answered, "God himself will provide the lamb for the burnt offering, my son." And the two of them went on together."

Sample Discovery Lesson #9

Solution in the New Testament

The purpose of this lesson:
1. Connect the Old Testament with the New Testament.
2. Compare between the sacrifices in the Old and New Testaments.
3. Remove the veil of the Old Testament by the coming of Christ.
4. Shows the way of salvation in Jesus as Lamb of God.

Read: John 1:1–18
Brief Overview of John 1:1–18

Sample Questions:

Q1. What does John 1–3 add to your perception of Genesis 1:1–3?

Q2. How was Jesus born? And who is his father?

Q3. How did Jesus use light to attract attention at his birth?

Q4. In verses 6–9, God sent John to the Jews to preach before the ministry of Christ. He had one main message. What was it? Explain John historically (mere prophet, but the greatest).

Q5. What was the purpose of John's ministry?

Sample Application Questions:
Q1. What do we learn about how a person can come to know God?

Q2. How would someone "full of grace and truth" treat others?

Sample Memory Verse(s):
John 1:29, NIV: "Jesus is the lamb of God who takes away the sin of the world"

John 1:14, NIV: "The word became flesh and made his dwelling among us. We have seen his glory, the glory of the One and Only, who came from the father, full of grace and truth."

CHAPTER 9

CONVERTING TO CHRISTIANITY— THE SHI'A EXPERIENCE

Generally, our Shi'a Muslim friends have no understanding of the goodness and character of the one true God. This is a process, and one that sometimes goes slowly. For a Muslim, it is sometimes shocking for them to see Islam with open eyes. In the light of Jesus Christ, its basic anti-Christian spirit becomes clear. During this process, Satan, or his followers, usually stir up people to threaten the new Muslim believers with fear of execution and physical harm.

Facing Realities

For Muslims to become Christians, they know well that it very possibly could mean rejection by their families and societies, losing their homes and jobs, being tortured and imprisoned or expelled from their countries, or even experiencing death in their home countries. Shi'a Muslims who convert to Christianity face a variety of reactions. These are some of the things my friends have told me they encountered when they called home to tell their parents:

1. Don't ever come home again. We will have to kill you if you do.
2. Come home, clear up all your personal affairs, and get out of this country.
3. There is no place here for you.

4. You may come home and retain your faith privately, if you promise not to share this with anyone.

As Christians, we must understand a Muslim's need for Christ, but in the same way, we need to understand his hesitation and fear for making the decision to follow Christ. We should ask ourselves if we are ready to stand with them and help them face the challenges. Former Muslims, upon becoming Christians, often struggle with having one foot in their former culture or faith. Through prayer, the Holy Spirit reveals such bondage and shows them the spirit of anti-Christ that is operating. They must take off the old cloth of Islam and put on the new cloth of Christ. They need to enter a new life that Jesus Christ provided for them in order to truly live for the first time. Muslim friends should separate themselves from their old practices and the habits remaining from their old lives, which opens doors for demonic footholds. For example, they should not continue to recite the Qur'an or pray in the name of Muhammad in order to "keep the peace" with their families.

1 Corinthians 6:19, NIV, says, "Do you not know that your body is a temple of the Holy Spirit, who is in you, whom you have received from God?" If someone hesitates and does not courageously follow Christ, it may mean that his or her new faith has not yet reached his or her heart. Continue to disciple and teach your new friend the truth. Encourage him or her to read the word, which will pierce his or her heart. Ask your friend to pray to God for courage and revelation. God will answer.

Seven Steps for Follow Up and Growth

1. The assurance of salvation

The most important thing after conversion is laying a proper foundation to ensure that our former Muslim friends who have Jesus Christ living in them are secure in their assurance of salvation and that they are saved by God's grace and not by their own deeds (Romans 10:9–10), that they have access to the forgiveness of sins (Ephesians 1:7), that God accepts them as his children (John 1:12–13), and that they possess eternal life (1John 5:11–13).

As Christians, we need to understand that it is not an easy thing for a Muslim to become a Christian, and we must trust and befriend him or her all the way. As the Muslim takes his or her first stunning steps as a baby Christian, he or she will stumble and fall—just like you did, more than once. It takes time and patience to raise a child and to be a parent, spiritually as well as physically. Maturity comes slowly. As our Lord has patience with us, so must we have patience with these "newborns." Help your friend to recognize his or her identify as a child of God and encourage him or her to build a personal relationship with God. Explain "quiet time," which will give him or her comfort, hope, and security for his or her future. God will reveal himself to those who sit with him (James 4:8; Proverb8:17; Psalm 34).

It has been estimated that among 50–70 percent of all Muslim converts return to Islam. Where has the failure been?

2. Stay close and encourage

The second step is maintaining a close relationship and following up one-on-one, and frequently doing so. It's important that your friends have someone to share with, to ask questions of, and from whom to witness a solid example of Christ. New converts quickly notice the weaknesses of other Christians around them. They see how the pastor preaches from the pulpit in a tone that's different from his or her reality and normal way of speaking.

Share with them the potential you see in them. Discover and discuss the specific goals they have. Assume a personal responsibility for the development of their goals. Discern the conflicts, which hinder the development of these goals. Suggest ways and means to help them achieve these goals. Be alert to scripture, which will encourage or guide them.

3. Character development

Ask them to share with you what they think are their own character strengths and weaknesses. Share your own. Encourage them regarding character strengths you see in them. Ask if they want you to help them overcome their character weaknesses, and then share how you have worked to overcome your own with God's strength. Be committed to faithfulness, loyalty, and availability. For example, in Islam, you are officially allowed to lie. If your friend still struggles with this, he or she needs to learn that it is not okay to lie. Do a "white lie or black lie" study with him or her through Ephesians 4:17–32, which illustrates that this is never acceptable.

4. Seek discipleship opportunities and conferences
Seek opportunities proactively for your friend to attend focused trainings and events that will help him or her grow in faith. Go with your friend where appropriate. Pray with him or her. Pray for anointing, and help him or her to walk by faith and to develop Christian leadership skills in accordance with his or her gifts.

5. Teach the two ordinances in the Bible
Specifically, teach them about water baptism and communion (the Lord's Supper). Teach him or her the value of fellowship with other Christians. Remember, Muslim people in general do not function well as individuals. They are closely connected to their families by flesh and blood, and by soul and custom. Abd al-Masih said, "They live as 'we' together with their relatives in line with the same principles, the same religion, and in a mutual responsibility for one another. Many were married or chosen for higher studies, or entered into influential positions in the government by decision of the clan. Without his family or clan the individual in the Orient is nothing and feels lost" (al-Masih 1993, 15).

6. Spiritual Gifts
Discuss spiritual gifts with them. Describe these in detail with examples and encourage them to seek out their gifts. Show them specific ways they can use these gifts, even early in their faith walk. This is an excellent way to help new converts get involved in serving within their faith communities and gain confidence. This will also help them gain an understanding of what God has called them to do and how he has specifically equipped them to do it.

Consider ways to train your friends to lead a small group. This will take some time, but it will give them meaning and purpose and will encourage them to study, learn, and grow in their faith. Also, should they return to their home countries, you will have equipped them to teach others who are walking a similar walk.

7. Encourage growth in biblical doctrine and application

Encourage new converts to study the word of God, grow through a bible study, and dive into a deep understanding of biblical doctrine and application. Provide them with resources that will be a good learning base. "The Bible is God's primary means through which He makes Himself and His will known to us (Hebrews 1:1–3). We must help our friends learn to feed on god's Word for themselves, so that they will not fall when they are alone because they have become too dependent on others" (al-Masih 1993, 38).

Chapter 9

Converting to Christianity—the Shi'a Experience

Discussion Questions:

1. Has your faith ever been challenged? Have you ever felt any kind of danger because of your beliefs? Please share.

2. How do you schedule or prioritize quiet times with the Lord? What has God taught you during your quiet times with him? Share as you feel led with the group.

3. When you were first saved, did anyone disciple or mentor you? What was the curriculum?

4. Early in your faith walk, what were some of the things that you found to be most helpful to grow and learn?

5. What are your spiritual gifts? How are you using them to advance the kingdom of God?

·· ❋ ··

CHAPTER 10

INPUT FROM THE FIELD

This appendix is based on an interview consisting of the same twelve questions posed to twenty different pastors and missionaries who work among Muslims in the United States. The purpose of these interviews was to gain input from their experiences while evangelizing to the Arabs and Iranian Shi'a. Through these interviews, I hoped to find more information about how these pastors approached the Shi'a with Christ's crucifixion and how these pastors communicated the message of the gospel of Jesus Christ to Shi'a Muslims in a North American context. These questions were also designed to investigate how these churches are crossing the cultural barriers in order to evangelize to the Shi'a Muslims. The following information contains the questions asked, along with the different answers I received from these pastors. I am going to put down their answers exactly as they responded. In chapter 10, I am going to summarize each response and turn it into a narrative synopsis.

1. When reaching Shi'a Muslims, does your approach differ from reaching other Muslims?
   a. No, I only use the Bible to witness, and that is good for everyone.
   b. No, in the beginning, I have the same approach. But if we get into deep issues, it would take a different slant from a Sunni Muslim.

c. Not really, except that I can appeal to the hero-concept of Jesus—like their Hussein, and the concept of "his blood was shed for us" that they promote at 'Ashurah (عشورة).

d. No, most are those who chose the direct and biblical way, but still, there were two respondents who prefer using illustrations and friendship.

e. No, I use more than one way.

f. Not really; however, some of the biblical responses to Sunni arguments are sidestepped when Shi'as say that the Sunnis have corrupted Islam. I think that, if workers had a better understanding of the doctrinal differences, we could avoid some of this; we could possibly be more effective in conveying the truth to them.

g. Yes, because most of the Shi'as that I know are not practicing Islam or really even considering themselves Muslim at this point. They seem to be significantly less convinced of the truth of Islam compared to Sunnis, and they are often leaning more toward secularism or even deism.

h. Yes, Shi'a Muslims are very in tune with the death of Hassan and Hussein. The tenth of Muharam is [a] very important religious activity for them. I try to capitalize on that event and relate it to the work of Christ. Many Shi'a will say that they remember Hassan and Hussein dying for them. They will say the Imam redeemed us. Or they will say we want to redeem the imam: *Fidak Ya Imam*, فداك يا امام"

i. No, developing genuine relationship with them, especially with those who are interested in spiritual things

2. What do you consider to be acceptable approaches in reaching Shi'a Muslims with the gospel?

   a. Shi'a tend to be more interested in spiritual topics than intellectual ones.

   b. First, friendship and hospitality are very important. Second, showing respect toward their culture, traditions, and history. Shiites are very aware of the civil wars that broke out in the early Islamic history, and they believe that they were persecuted. To sympathize with them, in issues of justice, wins them over. If those Shiites were Iranians, it would be easier because Iranians are disillusioned with Islam because of the grievances they've had since 1979. Third, a comparison between the martyrdom of Hussein and the vicarious nature of the cross would be helpful.

c. In general, I promote giving a New Testament and suggesting they read the gospel of John. Then we invite them to our ESL classes and social events to be around true believers and see God's love in action.

d. Love, Bible presentations, and prayer.

e. Just about anything provided, we are honest about wanting to see people saved and we genuinely love them. Most of what I have done in ministry has involved a typical "American" church-plant, direct evangelism, and teaching English. Much more could be done in the realm of social services, such as with job-training. It would also help to get them placed in sports.

f. I begin with friendship and look for ways to serve them. I also like to ask them about their beliefs. Then I usually affirm things that are in the Bible and give the biblical view for things that they say that contradict the Bible. From there, they usually ask some questions, and I am able to more fully present the gospel and compare and contrast Jesus in Christianity with Jesus in Islam.

g. Conversations where Christian ideas and thoughts are presented, biblical verses recited or discussed or shared with them over a cup of coffee. Biblical verse[s] used to share with them in a special situation, letting them see the movie *Jesus* or *Passion of Christ* [sic]. Give them a copy of the Injeel. Give them a book explaining why the Injeel is not corrupted.

h. Be honest and real.

i. Sharing my story with Jesus.

3. What are the top three difficulties that you face in evangelizing to Shi'a Muslims? How do you handle these difficulties?

a. I do not have any.

b. First, they need to understand that the Mahdi they await for is not the savior, but a worldly leader that won't save their souls. However, we avoid debate as much as we can. You may win a debate, but you will lose a friend. Second, it needs a lot of diplomacy to explain that Ali and the Imams from his bloodline are just sinners like us, and we have to keep our eyes fixed on Christ. Third, we have to make Shiites tolerate other Sunni seekers. In the beginning, it may need separation between the two parties.

c. They're too busy, so I keep inviting connection points, as above. They're so stuck in conforming to the community, so I must respect it and bridge to others. They're not good about reading anything, much less the NT, so I offer to read together or just talk informally.

d. It takes a long time, and you just need to keep plodding even when they reject your message.

e. Lack of genuine interest in spiritual matters, family pressure, and a lack of understanding their mind-set. I handle this by prayer, evangelizing broadly and persistently, study of appropriate literature, and spending time with people.

f. Many of them feel dissatisfied with Shi'ism and therefore don't want any further religion.

g. There is a definite stigma attached to Christianity, so this keeps people at arm's length from Jesus in the Bible. There are many stereotypes and prejudices to overcome. There is much inaccurate information on both Islam and the Bible/Christianity. I try to get them to read the Bible. I am hoping to start meeting with Muslims to compare the Qur'an and the Bible as a way of getting them more into scripture. I also try to talk with them through these various difficulties to help them see another perspective.

h. Family pressures—allegiance for the family or clan. Political pressures going after political alliance. Victim mentality—Shi'a are less than Muslims—we are oppressed, all these create a hindrance for them to respond.

i. They believe the Bible is incorrect, feel Christians [are] pro-Israel and [have a] fear of Islam. To handle these difficulties, persuade Arab Shi'a to read the Bible, strongholds and prayers.

4. To evangelize to Shi'a Muslims, what setting do you prefer: an "individual" (one on one) or a "group setting"?

   a. Always individually.

   b. One-on-one is the best approach.

   c. Oh, one to one, by far! That's my strength, by God's grace.

   d. It takes a long time and you just need to keep plodding even when they reject your message.

   e. Group setting. One Muslim and twenty loving Christians.

   f. It depends on the situation—both are valid.

   g. I prefer one-on-one setting, as it is easier to keep on track and move the discussion toward Jesus.

   h. I like the one-on-one, although the group setting is a good way to start.

   i. People from Muslim descendent should be seen as authority figure [sic]. One-on-one man basis.

5. What biblical topic do you usually begin with when presenting the gospel to Shi'a?

   a. Story of Abraham.

   b. The vicarious act of Jesus on the cross. Evidence from historians like Josephus is good.

   c. That we get to heaven by God's mercy, not by our works.

   d. Comparing the Qur'anic and biblical paradise.

   e. The gospel of John is on the top (because of John 3:16), and the story of Nicodemus, which is useful for the pious Shi'a Muslims. John 4 is used for explaining who the true worshippers are, and it is used for people who feel guilty and need to find the way of forgiveness. Muslims feel guilty even if they are performing the five pillars. It is the action of the Holy Spirit that leads some of them to feel guilty and search for forgiveness. Luke 15 is used for the Parable of the Lost Son. It is useful for some youths who have feelings similar to that of the younger son. Surprisingly, no one used Luke 24, of the two disciples on the Emmaus Road, although it could be used as seen in chapter 7.

   f. The story of the cross, as found in the gospels, was useful because of its historicity and details. It has the power to attract searchers for the truth. Jesus was whipped so you don't have to whip yourself for ten days every year. No, actually, I start with letting ʿAbbas Al-Salami, whose family is from Najif, Iraq experience the love he never had at home from his Shiʾa parents. The story of Abraham.

g. It depends on the situation—both are valid.

h. I start with God as [a] creature who entered into creation and then speak about the person and work of Jesus and the story of Abraham.

i. Followed by the correctness of the gospel.

6. Which biblical references, stories, illustrations, or analogies do you think are useful to explain the cross to Shiʾas?

a. I like to use the parables of Jesus.

b. Every person is different. The Prodigal Son is good. But when they start comparing, the Shahada of Hussein in Karbala could be compared to the death of Jesus on the cross.

c. We offer the Jesus film, and gospel John to read. I took a few Shiʾas to see "The Passion" film that year!

d. The story of Abraham's sacrifice and the sacrifice of ʿId al-Adha are the most illustrative for use in explaining the death of Christ. The Qurʾan says, "We ransomed him with a momentous sacrifice" (Sura 37: 107). Refer to the sacrifices of Moses.

e. A creative illustration by saying that the plants must be eaten (sacrificed) for the life of the animals, and animals must be eaten for the life of the humans. How can we sacrifice the life of a human except by sacrificing a more precious life? The life of Jesus was the only way to sacrifice a human.

f. The parable of Jesus.

g. Genesis 3 (Adam and Eve sinning, along with the promise of the Messiah in verse 15 and God clothing them with animal skins).

h. Abraham offering his son as a sacrifice but replacing him with an animal instead. Lazarus. Genesis 22 (Abraham offering his son and God providing a ram—we as sinners deserve to die, but Jesus died in our place). Abraham, the "friend of God," using this as a bridge to explain how we can become friends of God by faith in Jesus. Share my testimony.

    i.   The sacrifice of Abraham, the Prodigal Son, and the workers in the vineyard.

7. How should the death of Christ be presented to draw the Shi'a Muslim's attention to Christ?

    a.   Using the story of Abraham, I explain the need for sacrifice. I have used the example of a judge that sentences the criminal to pay a big fine, then gets down and writes a check to pay it.

    b.   As an act, not only vicarious, but also that brings justice to a fallen world system. Shi'a Islam has a grievance against Sunni Islam. So justice is a relevant issue.

    c.   We offer the Jesus film, and go. John to read. I took a few Shi'as to see "The Passion" film that year!

    d.   One said that [he] was impressed with the records of Christ's miracles. He was greatly affected by John 3:16.

    e.   As the fulfillment of OT prophecies, the fulfillment of the Passover Lamb, the deaths of Ali and Hussein as a way to convey the idea of someone offering up one's life for others, although I prefer to use Genesis 22.

    f.   I think that Jesus's death needs to be shown as a willing sacrifice on our behalf because of a loving God.

    g.   The substitutionary work of Christ on the cross presentation. Sacrificing oneself for the sake of many. Sacrifice to free people from slavery. Hussein died for they wanted freedom from oppression. Christ died to release us from slavery to sin.

    h.   Comparing the Qur'anic and biblical verses of Christ's death and life.

    i.   Lay down your life for them. Sacrifice your time.

8. What was Shi'a attitude (positive or negative) toward the cross?

    a.   I have not found Shi'as argue about the cross as much as Sunnis. But it is always the same: that Jesus did not die.

    b.   It differs—many refuse to accept that Jesus died. However, they grasp the idea better than Sunni Muslims.

    c.   They've been told that it didn't happen, so only the Spirit can break through that lie!

d. Most of these Shi'a Muslims believed that Christians worship the cross, but there was a sizable number who thought that it was a symbol of love for Christians.

e. The category with the highest percentage had the barrier of considering the cross as idolatry and falsehood. Even those who considered the cross as a symbol of love and something for blessing were not recognizing the real power and meaning of the cross as Muslims.

f. Several Shi'a have told me that they believe Jesus died on the cross; yet, they still argue that he was not crucified.

g. It is very difficult for them to grasp, and I think that they need to hear about the cross several times before they even begin to consider it.

h. The negative comes on the concept that Jesus the prophet of God lost. This is where it needs to be connected with the resurrection.

i. Mostly consider the cross as a symbol of Christianity and crusaders.

9. What were the most influential reason(s) that turned Shi'as' lives around to accept Christ?

a. Dreams and visions of Jesus.

b. Maybe the harshness of life in the Middle East under ruthless dictators.

c. In Dearborn, we only have one recent example of an Iraqi Shi'a coming to Jesus, but several Lebanese Shi'a. I'd say the key reason is seeing the love of believers in action! God loves me; therefore, he sacrificed his son for me.

d. The Bible is true and better. The most influential reason was that the Bible gave the final words of God. The validity of the Bible is important because the Muslim objections can be answered through reading the Bible. Then came another seven who found the assurance of forgiveness as the most influential message in turning their lives to accept Christ. Chose that Jesus is still alive, which is an Islamic thought and can be used as a bridge in communicating the gospel.

e. Jesus's character must be clarified to Shi'a Muslims to set the stage for accepting the gospel.

f. The study Arabic literature, he discovered that there were enlightening analogies of that expression. For example, in the Qur'an itself, there is the term *Ibn as-sabil* (ابن السبيل), which is literally *son of the path*. One will also find the expression *son of Satan*. It is obvious that these are metaphorical forms of expression and do not involve physical reproduction. But these meaningful terms indicate some relationship and character. Al-ka'aba is called "the mother of the town [of Mecca]." In a similar way, the title "the Son of God" indicates a unique relationship between God and Christ, not any process of procreation. Love.

g. The conviction of the Holy Spirit in conjunction with hearing/reading the Bible; persistent and loving witness of Christians; some supernatural witness that shows them the power of Jesus Christ.

h. Hearing the gospel presented several times by a friend who is living out the teaching of Jesus.

i. The life of the Christians friends they met; the presentation of the basic beliefs of Christianity; vision and dreams of Jesus.

10. What is the most critical area of change your church must embrace in order to evangelize to the Shi'a Muslims?

a. To welcome them and not ignore them.

b. Human care, benevolence, immigration services.

c. Get out of your warm "cocoon" and reach out to the lost. They're not even doing that within their own culture!

d. Learn Arabic better.

e. The church we attend does witness and evangelize. In general, though, we all need to evangelize more. A greater conviction of our personal responsibility to witness along with "church-wide" types of opportunities to witness.

f. I think that the small-group aspect needs to really become strong and central to how the church works. I think that it would be easier for a Shi'a to see Christ in a small-group setting than during Sunday worship service.

g. Love Shi'a Muslims, train themselves on witnessing, create avenues where they can meet Muslims, and share with them one on one.

h. Have a heart and passion to see them come to Jesus—step out in faith.

i. American women are afraid of how Muslim men treat women. Educate Christian members about Islam and Muslim Shi'a belief and culture. Courage, trust, and humility showed by welcoming and hosting.

11. By which way were the Shi'a Muslims most attracted to your church?

a. Shi'a Muslims come to church and they [are] impressed by the joy expressed.

b. Friendship, compassion, respect, migration services.

c. I don't advocate them coming to church—too much cultural confusion. The men come to look at the women! Let them see believers of the same gender—in class or at parties.

d. Love.

e. Personal friendships with those who invited them.

f. Personal invitation by friend.

g. Friendships with members of the church family. Reading the New Testament and asking questions.

h. Diversity in the church and hospitality events.

i. Community, food, prayer, and men's and women's groups.

12. What kind of environment does your church offer to Shi'a Muslims?

a. Social dinners and home fellowships.

b. Tolerance, respect of their previous beliefs, culture, and identity. Focusing on faith, contextualization of the gospel, and not Christian traditions.

c. We have an Arabic fellowship, but it's not culturally sensitive, in my opinion.

d. Intentional love of Muslims.

e. A caring and loving environment.

f.   There is significant community for them, but I think that there are probably several barriers to the gospel when Shi'a first comes to church on Sunday morning.

g.   One-on-one discipleship. Worship services. Fellowship dinners.

h.   We are very giving and help people out in lots of practical and loving ways—though we can always improve.

i.   Crossing the cultural barriers. Creating a close enough connect so they will listen to me. Discipleship, bible study, small family-oriented church.

·◦·❋·◦·

CHAPTER 11

BOOK INTERVIEW EVALUATION

In this chapter, I will summarize, evaluate, and explain the responses of the pastors' and missionaries' interview for Muslims. These workers have worked hard with Muslims, particularly among Shi'a Muslims, and have experienced God's work in the Muslims; lives. The questions and the specific data of the interview respondents can be found in appendix 6.

According to question one, 80 percent of the Christian workers among Muslims believed reaching Shi'a Muslims was no different from approaching other Muslims. Only 20 percent said there was a difference. The belief was that the difference was because Shi'a Muslims were not participants of Islam and were loyal to the death of Hassan and Hussein. (It is possible that the 20 percent probably know more about the Sunni and Shi'a beliefs and history.)

According to question two, most pastors chose the direct and biblical way. The reason for this approach shows that the person ministering to the Arab honestly wanted to see people saved and wanted others to see that they are genuinely loved. Yet there were still a few respondents who preferred using illustrations and friendship.

According to question three, the top difficulties faced in evangelism are 1) a lack of time for building relationships with Shi'a Muslims (we prefer confronting them with the gospel and debating them more than winning their friendship); 2) the need for diplomacy, wisdom, and knowledge to explain that Ali and the Imams are just sinners and that they need Christ; and 3) a lack of understanding of the Arab Shi'a mind-set. There is a need to learn about their cultures, languages, and beliefs. One way to handle that is to offer our practical love, the word of God, and to pray.

According to question four, more than 80 percent of Christian workers say they prefer one-on-one relationships with Shi'a Muslims (natural evangelism or indirect evangelism). Fewer than 20 percent of Christian workers prefer a group setting for evangelism. Shi'a Muslims hear about Christ through attending a church. These Arab Shi'a Muslims go to a church through an invitation to a wedding ceremony or a funeral, Christians holidays, occasions, and other similar church events. Many went to a church and were witnessed to through friends who brought them to revival meetings. Therefore, we should invite them to church events in order to give them the chance of overcoming the barrier of entering a church.

According to question five, most Christian workers say Arab Shi'a Muslims came to Christ through direct evangelism, reading the Bible, or a book about the authenticity of the Bible. For the Arab Shi'a Muslim, the question of the reliability of the Bible arose often. The most influential argument was that the Bible gave the final word of God; therefore, putting the Bible in every hand is important because it can give the answers to the Arab Shi'a Muslims' questions and it can facilitate communicating the message of the Cross. Many biblical topics can be useful for reaching Muslims. For example, the story of Abraham and the story of the cross, as found in the gospels, were useful because of their historicity and details (Al-Adha and 'Ashoura). Both have the power to attract Shi'a Muslim seekers of the truth.

Other biblical topics that rated high were the gospel of John (John 3:16) and the story of Nicodemus (John 3), which is useful for the pious Shi'a Muslims. The story of the Samaritan women at the well (John 4) is used for explaining who the true worshippers are, and it is used for people who feel guilty and need to find the way of forgiveness. Muslims feel guilty even if they are performing the five pillars. It is the action of the Holy Spirit that leads some of them to search for forgiveness. Luke 15 is used for the parable of the lost son and is useful for some youths who have stories like that of the younger son. The character of Jesus Christ after watching a movie of Jesus passion or learning any other thing about Jesus's doings and that we get to heaven by God's mercy, not by our works, is also helpful in reaching Muslims.

According to question six, biblical references, stories, illustrations, or analogies are useful for explaining the cross to Shi'as. One responded, "The Prodigal Son is good." Comparing the martyr (*Shahada* or شهادة) of Hussein in Karbala could be compared with the death of Jesus on the cross. They also like to use the parable of Jesus. One of the respondents referred to the sacrifices of Moses. One gave a creative illustration by saying that the plants must be eaten (sacrificed) for the lives of the animals, and animals must be eaten for the lives of the humans. How can we sacrifice the life of a human except by sacrificing a more precious life? The life of Jesus was the only way to sacrifice a human. Two respondents used Genesis 3 (Adam and Eve sinning, along with the promise of the Messiah in verse 15, and God clothing them with animal skins). One respondent shared his testimony. As an act, the cross was not only victorious, but it also brought justice to a fallen world system. Shi'a Islam has a grievance against Sunni Islam, so justice is a relevant issue. Some would like to offer the Jesus movie and go. John to read. I took a few Shi'as to see the movie *The Passion of the Christ*, and one of them said that he was impressed with the records of Christ's miracles. He was greatly affected by John 3:16. One of the respondents said, "I prefer to use Genesis 22."

According to question seven, most of the Christian workers maintained that the story of Abraham's sacrifice and the sacrifice of 'Id al-Adha (الاضحى عيد) are the most illustrative for use in explaining the death of Christ. It shows how Abraham was a "friend of God" and then shows how we can become friends of God by faith in Jesus. The power of the cross was great evidence for converts, especially when it was used for exorcism or when it appeared as a sign. Shi'a Muslims are deeply affected by dreams and visions. Some Muslims have been affected by supernatural powers. There is a great need to pray for them in the name of Christ for performing a miracle or exorcism, using the power of his blood. Some Shi'a Muslims are affected by the Qur'anic verses about Christ. Compare the Qur'anic and biblical paradise. Technology and media could be used to give a clear message about Christ's crucifixion and resurrection.

According to question eight, the Shi'a Muslims' attitude toward the cross, according to the interview, showed the following: Shi'a Muslims do not argue about the cross as much as Sunnis. Shi'as grasp the idea of the cross better than Sunni Muslims. Many Shi'a believe Jesus died on the cross; yet, they still argue that he was not crucified. But it is always the same result: Jesus did not die. Idolatry was the greatest cause for difficulty with the cross. Even those who considered the cross as a symbol of love and something for blessing did not recognize the real power and meaning of the cross.

According to question nine, Christian workers say the most influential reason(s) that turned the Shi'a's life around to accept Christ were dreams and visions of Jesus and maybe the harshness of life in the Middle East under ruthless dictators. Most answers pointed to one key reason: seeing the love of believers in action. God loves me; therefore, he sacrificed his son for me. The most influential reason was the fact that Jesus was still alive, which is an Shi'a thought that can be used as a bridge in communicating the gospel. Jesus's character must be clarified to Shi'a Muslims in order to set the stage for accepting the gospel.

According to question ten, Christian workers say the most critical area of change your church must embrace is to welcome the Shi'a Muslims and not ignore them. The church should have human care, benevolence, and immigration services. It must get out of its comfort zone and step out in faith. It must learn about Shi'a culture, language, and faith. They're not even doing that within their own cultures. And finally, the church must destroy the fearful stereotype of Islam.

According to question eleven, Christian workers say Shi'a Muslims are most attracted to your church when they see the joy expressed through worship. They are also attracted by the friendship, love, compassion, respect, and immigration services. Some Christian workers responded by saying they didn't advocate for them coming to church, as it causes too much cultural confusion. The men come to look at the women. Let them see believers of the same gender in class or at parties.

According to the last question, Christian workers say the kind of environment that your church offers to Shi'a Muslims should cross cultural barriers by having social dinners and home fellowships. The church must be tolerant and respectful of previous beliefs, cultures, and identities. The church also has to focus on faith, contextualization of the gospel, and not just Christian traditions. One responded that the church should have intentional love and a caring environment.

In conclusion, 25 percent of Christian workers say Shi'a Muslims came to Christ through indirect evangelism: hospitality, hosting, hearing Christian radio, seeing Christ through the life of some Christians, being treated in a Christian clinic or hospital, and being in Christian schools.

There are many factors that can help build sociological bridges with Shi'a Muslims. Social work and medical work can prepare the soil for communicating the atoning work of Christ. Only 10 percent of Christian workers say Shi'a Muslims accepted the cross as a historical fact, and others became convinced through comparative religion studies. Apologetic study is useful for some knowledgeable seekers of the truth. Therefore, it can be used wisely without aggressive attack. Some Shi'a Muslims are affected by the Qur'anic verses about Christ. In addition, the Qur'an gives more general recommendations for presenting the atoning death of Christ in different ways. The fundamental Muslims make a stronger defense than other Muslims. They have their reason: they are obeying God. The Qur'an says, "Fight those who believe neither in God nor the Last Day ... nor acknowledge the Religion of Truth" (Sura 9:29). They have their special interpretations of this verse, which, in their eyes, justifies their actions. Their attitude is reflected in their relations with Christians.

Sixty-five percent of Christian workers say Shi'a Muslims accepted Christ through a direct way of evangelism, by preaching, sharing biblical stories, reading the Bible, or seeing dreams, visions, and miracles. Media is a very effective vehicle for gospel proclamation. Teaching the difficult questions that Muslims usually ask about Christ requires patience and time. Shi'a Muslims usually ask about sin, Christ's redemption, and the cross.

REFERENCES

Al-Masih, Abd. 1995. *The Great Deception*. Villach, Austria: Light of Life.

———. 1996. *The Main Challenges for Committed Christians in serving Muslims*. Villach, Austria: Light of Life.

———. 2002. *Should Every Muslim who Becomes a Christian Die?* Weirton, WV
USA: Grace and Truth.

———. 2003. *Islamic Marriage*. Weirton, WV
USA: Grace and Truth.

———. 2003. *The Great Commission of Jesus our Lord*. 2nd ed. Weirton, WV
USA: Grace and Truth.

Abi-Hashem, forthcoming. Arab Americans: Understanding their challenges, needs, and struggles. In A. Marsella, P. Watson, F. Norris, J. Johnson, and J. Gryczynski (Eds.), *Ethnocultural guidebook for disasters and trauma: A primer for responders and service providers*. Publisher: Springer-Verlag (or) Kluwer-Plenum.

Accad, Fouad E. 1997. *Building Bridges: Christianity and Islam*. Colorado Springs: Navpress.

Acord, Bud. 1994. *Muslim Friends*. Colorado Springs: Al-Nour Publishers.

Al-Jadeed, Iskander and Irsaneous. 1990. *Hatmiyyat al-Kaffara* [The necessity for the atonement]. Cairo: Evangelical Theological Seminary.

Ankerberg, John and John Weldon. 2001. *Fast Facts on Islam: What You Need to Know Now*. Eugene, Oregon: Harvest House.

Association of Church Missions Commissions Newsletter. Autumn, 1989.

Habib Badr, chief editor; Suad Abou el Rouss Slim, assistant editor ; Joseph Abou Nohra, assistant editor, 2005. *Christianity: A History in the Middle East*. Beirut, Lebanon: The Middle East Council of Churches.

Berley, James D. 1986. *Preaching to Convince*. Waco, Tex: Word Books.

Bewley, Aisha. 1998. *Glossary of Islamic Terms*. Ta-Ha Publishers Ltd. (UK). Bosch, David J. 1991. *Transforming Mission: Paradigm Shifts in Theology of Mission.* New York: Orbis Books.

Caner, Ergun Mehmet and Emir F. Caner. 2002. *Unveiling Islam*. Grand Rapids: Kregel Publications.

Cleveland, William L. 2000. *A History of the Modern Middle East*. 2nd ed. Boulder, CO: Westview Press.

Delong-Bas, Natana J. 2004. *Wahhabi Islam: From Revival and Reform to Global Jihad*. Oxford: Oxford University Press.

Engel, James F. and William A. Dyrness. 2000. *Changing the Mind of Missions: Where Have We Gone Wrong*. Downers Grove, Illinois: Intervarsity.

Farah, Caesar E. 1994. *Islam: Beliefs and Observances*. San Diego, CA, U.S.A: Barron's.

Gabriel, Mark A. 2002. *Islam and Terrorism*. Lake Mary, Florida, USA: Charisma House.

Geisler, Norman and Frank Turek. Crossway Books, 2004. *I Don't Have Enough Faith to Be an Atheist.*

Graham, Billy, Leighton Ford, Luis Palau, Roberts E. Coleman. 1989. *Choose Ye This Day. How to Effectively Proclaim the Gospel Message.* Woodbury, MN: Llewellyn Worldwide Minnesota Publication.

Haneef, Suzanne. 1996. *What Everyone Should Know About Islam and Muslims.* Chicago, IL USA: Library of Islam.

Harik, Judith Palmer. 2005. *Hezbollah: The Changing Face of Terrorism.* London: I.B. Tauris.

Hiebert, Paul G. and Eloise Hiebert Meneses. 1995. *Incarnational Ministry: Planting Churches in Band, Tribal, Peasant, and Urban Societies.* Grand Rapids, MI: Baker Books

Kosezegi, Michael A. and J. Gordon Melton. 1992. *Islam In North America: A Sourcebook.* New York: Garland Publishing.

Lingenfelter, Sherwood G. and Marvin K. Mayers. 1986. *Ministering Cross-Culturally: An Incarnational Model for Personal Relationships.* Grand Rapids, MI: Baker Book House.

Lloyd-Jones, Martyn D. 1971. *Preaching and Preachers.* Grand Rapids, MI: Zondervan.

Love, Rick. 2000. *Muslims Magic And the Kingdom of God.* Pasadena, CA: William Carey Library.

Malconson, William L. 1969. *The Preaching Event.* Philadelphia: Westminster Press.

Maxwell, John C. 1993. *Developing the Leader Within You.* Nashville: Thomas Nelson Publishing.

McCurry, Don. 2001. *Healing the Broken Family of Abraham: New Life for Muslims*. Colorado Springs: Ministries to Muslims.

McDowell, Bruce A. and Anees Zaka. 1999. *Muslims and Christians at the Table: Promoting Biblical Understanding Among North American Muslims*. Harmony Township, NJ: Presbyterian & Reformed Publishing.

Mehmet, Ergun and Emir F. Caner. 2002. *Unveiling Islam*. Grand Rapids: Kregel Publications.

Mikhail, Labib. 1996. *Islam, Muhammad and the Koran*. Example Product Manufacturer; USA. United States.

Miller, Roland E. 1995. *Muslim Friends their Faith and Feeling: An Introduction to Islam*. St. Louis, MO: Concordia Publishing House.

Mirza, Nate. 1993. *Home Again*. Zondervan Publishing House.

Neusner, Jacob., ed., 2006. *Religious Foundations of Western Civilization: Judaism, Christianity, and Islam*. Nashville: Abingdon Press.

Phillips, Tom, Bob Norsworthy, and W. Terry Whalin. 1997. *The World at Your Door*. Minneapolis: Bethany House.

Poston, Larry A. and Carl F. Ellis Jr. 2000. *The Changing Face of Islam in America: Understanding And Reaching Your Muslim Neighbor.* Philadelphia: Horizon Books.

Rhodes, Ron. 2002. *Reasoning from the Scriptures with Muslims*. Eugene, OR: Harvest House.

Rizvi, Akhtar and Syed S. Rizvi. 1985. *Islam: Faith, Practice, and History Imamat: The Vicegerence of the Prophet*. Tehran: WOFIS.

Ruthven, Malise. 1984. *Islam in The World*. New York: Oxford University Press.

Saad-Ghorayeb, Amal. 2002. *Hizbu'allah Politics and Religion*. London: Pluto Press.

Shorrosh, Anis. 1988. *Islam Revealed*. Nashville: Thomas Nelson.

Taqi al-Hakim, Muhammad and Abdul Hadi As-Sayyid. "Migration to Non-Muslim Countries: General Rules." Accessed January 26, 1998.

Wagner, Peter C. 1992. *Warfare Prayer*. Ventura, CA: Regal Books.

Watt, Montgomery W. 1963. *Muslim Intellectual: A Study of al-Ghazali*. Edinburgh: University Press.

Winter, Raalph D. and Steven C. Hawthorn. 1999. *Perspectives on the World Christian Movement*, Carlisle, England: Paternoster.

Wuthnow, Robert, ed. 1998. *Encyclopedia of Politics and Religion*, vol 2. Washington, DC: Congressional Quarterly.

Printed in the United States
By Bookmasters